European Vernacular Literacy

NEW PERSPECTIVES ON LANGUAGE AND EDUCATION
Series Editor: Professor Viv Edwards, *University of Reading, Reading, Great Britain*
Series Advisor: Professor Allan Luke, *Queensland University of Technology, Brisbane, Australia*

Two decades of research and development in language and literacy education have yielded a broad, multidisciplinary focus. Yet education systems face constant economic and technological change, with attendant issues of identity and power, community and culture. This series will feature critical and interpretive, disciplinary and multidisciplinary perspectives on teaching and learning, language and literacy in new times.

Full details of all the books in this series and of all our other publications can be found on http://www.multilingual-matters.com, or by writing to Multilingual Matters, St Nicholas House, 31–34 High Street, Bristol BS1 2AW, UK.

NEW PERSPECTIVES ON LANGUAGE AND EDUCATION
Series Editor: Professor Viv Edwards, University of Reading, Reading, Great Britain

European Vernacular Literacy
A Sociolinguistic and Historical Introduction

Joshua A. Fishman

MULTILINGUAL MATTERS
Bristol • Buffalo • Toronto

Library of Congress Cataloging in Publication Data
A catalog record for this book is available from the Library of Congress.
Fishman, Joshua A.
European Vernacular Literacy: A Sociolinguistic and Historical Introduction/
Joshua A. Fishman.
New Perspectives on Language and Education
Includes bibliographical references and index.
1. English language--Variation--Europe. 2. English language--Study and teaching--Europe. 3. Languages in contact. 4. Linguistic change. I. Title.
PE2751.F54 2010
306.44089–dc22 2010021279

British Library Cataloguing in Publication Data
A catalogue entry for this book is available from the British Library.

ISBN-13: 978-1-84769-292-4 (hbk)
ISBN-13: 978-1-84769-291-7 (pbk)

Multilingual Matters
UK: St Nicholas House, 31–34 High Street, Bristol, BS1 2AW, UK.
USA: UTP, 2250 Military Road, Tonawanda, NY 14150, USA.
Canada: UTP, 5201 Dufferin Street, North York, Ontario, M3H 5T8, Canada.

Copyright © 2010 Joshua A. Fishman.

All rights reserved. No part of this work may be reproduced in any form or by any means without permission in writing from the publisher.

The policy of Multilingual Matters/Channel View Publications is to use papers that are natural, renewable and recyclable products, made from wood grown in sustainable forests. In the manufacturing process of our books, and to further support our policy, preference is given to printers that have FSC and PEFC Chain of Custody certification. The FSC and/or PEFC logos will appear on those books where full certification has been granted to the printer concerned.

Typeset by Techset Composition Ltd., Salisbury, UK.

Elyinken, Noamken, Shai-li Reyzelen, Un Sonyelen	עלינקען, נועמקען, שי-לי רייזעלען, און סאניעלען:
Fir neshomelekh	פיר נשמהלעך
vemen ikh hob tsu fardanken mayn tsveyte yungshaft!	וועמען איך האב צו פארדאנקען מיין צווייטע יונגשאפט!
Halevay zol yidish bay aykh lebn un zikh redn, leyenen un zingen gring un hanoedik!	הלוואי זאל ייִדיש ביי אייך לעבן און זיך רעדן, לייענען און זינגען גרינג און הנאהדיק!
Far aykh alemen a mantonele Funem gantsn hartsn!	פאר אייך אלעמען א מתנהלע פונעם גאנצן הארצן!

(Translation of dedication)

To Elyinke, Noam, Shai-Li Reyzelele and Sonye-Elena,
Four new souls who have given me
My second childhood

May Yiddish live within them
And may speaking, reading and singing it
Flow easily and happily from within them!

A gift for all of you
With all my heart!

Contents

1. Why Has Interest in Languages and Literacies Increased So Much Lately? 1
2. What is a 'Language' of Vernacular Literacy? 5
   A Dictionary Definition 5
   Another Approach 6
   Scalability: Attributes That Presuppose Others 14
3. The Rise of Vernaculars of Literacy in Europe. 19
   Introducing Karl W. Deutsch (1912–1992) and Time 1 (T1) 19
   Time 2 (T2): 1250 C.E. and the Next Few
      Centuries Thereafter 21
   Time 3 (T3): 1800 C.E. 27
   Time 4 (T4): 1900 28
   Times 5 and 6 (T5 and T6) (1937 and 1990) 28
   Toward Understanding Some of the Essential
      Society-wide Characteristics of Literacy 30
4. Macro-factors in the Societal Spread of Vernacular Literacy 37
   Religions of Literacy 37
   Widespread Sociocultural Change in Nonreligious Pursuits 40
   The West to East Trajectory in the Rise of
      Vernacular Languages of Literacy 45
   The Role of the Spread of Religion, Philosophy and
      Style of Life in the Rise of New Languages 46
   The Dampening Effect of a Much Stronger and Already
      Widely Known Neighbor That Is Very Similar to Its
      Weaker Cognate 48
5. Heroes of European Vernacular Literacy 51
   Antonio de Nebrija (1441–1522) 51
   Johann Gutenberg (1390[?]–1468) 53

'Vuk' (Vuk Stefanovic Karadzic): (1787–1864) 56
Mendl Lefin (1749–1826) 60
Concluding Reflections on the Four Horsemen of
European Vernacular Literacy 64

6   Micro-factors in the Societal Spread of Vernacular Literacy 66
    Elitist Literacy and Its Outgrowths 66
    A 'Chicken and Egg' Problem 69
    The Elephant in the Room: The Growth in Parsimonious
    Communicational Possibilities 70
    Summary 71

7   The 'Literacy Bullies on the Block' 73
    The Exportation of English Literacy and of
    Indigenous Vernacular Literacy to the Anglosphere 73
    A Brief Comparison with Vernacular Literacies in
    the Francophone Sphere................................. 79
    Other European Vernaculars as Competitors with
    Local Vernacular Literacies Elsewhere..................... 80

8   Vernacular Literacy for What?................................ 84
    The Road to Heaven is Littered with Good Intentions 85

Index 87

Chapter 1
Why Has Interest in Languages and Literacies Increased So Much Lately?

'Language watchers', such as writers, intelligent readers, linguists, teachers, journalists and literary critics, and even ordinary educated citizens and writers of 'letters to the editor' of their local newspapers, have increasingly noted that English has been changing before their very eyes. In some circles a construction such as 'between you and I', which is heard so frequently in casual speech, is considered to be perfectly OK even in print. Others will accept it as being correct only in some contexts but not in others. Still others will not accept it at all. 'Things change' may seem to us to be an obvious observation, but few of us stop to think that just four or five centuries ago, even English as a whole was not considered appropriate for written or for printed purposes by the best educated and most literate segments of English society. Before we decide whether this latter change (namely the eminently 'print-worthy' nature of English in practically everyone's eyes) was a good or bad development, let us pause to suspend judgment and first to inquire how, where and when such changes occurred, whether they also occurred with other languages and, indeed, whether they are still occurring to certain languages today. Indeed, answering the latter questions may actually give us some better perspective on how to evaluate 'between you and I' and to understand why many (most?) of those who would employ the latter construction would never consider 'between you and we' or 'between you and they' as acceptable, whether in print or in speech. Furthermore, even if we accept that English is changing rapidly in some respects, for some 'users' (speakers/writers), and in certain functions (e.g. newspaper articles but not in State of the Nation addresses), we must also quickly admit that some features of English have remained quite change-resistant, even obdurately so, in ways that many would characterize as self-punitive (e.g. its wide departure from regular sound–letter correspondences). Of course, beauty is in the eye of the beholder, but there cannot be many 'great' languages out there in which the simple 'oo'-sound (as in moo!) is also spelled 'ue' (as in 'true'), 'ough' (as in 'through'), 'ew' (as in 'flew') and just plain 'o' (as in 'who'). It is a wonder that anyone learns how to read and write a language as orthographically inconsistent as that!

The latter issue is even more basically related to the rise of vernacular literacy, the basic topic of this brief book, than is the former one which is concerned 'merely' with the 'correctness judgments' for a particular grammatical form. Actually, however, we will ultimately see that both of these issues are strongly related to each other and to our underlying theme, because they are both aspects of 'standardization', without which no accomplished literacy nor enduring greatness judgments are possible. Standardization requires the acceptance of authoritative deciders in questions of language as well as disciplined acceptors of that authority. The coming into being of either of these authority-related dramatis personae may take centuries to develop and even when they both already are in place, 'it moves nevertheless' (i.e. the language continues to change since variability is part of the human condition per se), at least as long as the language is alive. Clearly this book is about a difficult adventure: to attempt to tame the living and yet to keep it alive, creative and truly human. Literacy is surrounded on both sides: by too little standardization on the one hand and by too much on the other. There is no way of avoiding criticism for those engaged in literacy efforts. No matter what it is that they do, they are unavoidably damned by some if they do and damned by others if they don't.

Returning to our very first observation, namely that interest in languages and literacies has increased of late, we may also want to ask why this may be so. Several possible reasons come to mind. Perhaps it is in part attributable to the increased expansion of our capacity to identify with and be curious about peoples and cultures that were formerly out of sight and out of mind. Such increases in the 'range of interest' are characteristic of growth in 'modernization of the mind' and of the expansion of contacts between segments of our own population, its minorities included, not to mention contacts with populations all over the world. We have also become more alert to the value of biodiversity and to its fragility, due to the impact of growing industrialization and commercialization all over the world and in our own midst. This has all gone on together with (and perhaps because of) an increased awareness of our own interdependence on other peoples and other languages. We may no longer be as certain as we once were that we are inherently better than they are, either intellectually or morally, but this also makes us more appreciative of what we truly are and value.

The English language is one of the greatest and most prized possessions of the anglophone world, so those of us who are members of this world, directly or indirectly, should want to know more about it and not take it for granted, even though only a few centuries ago it was no more widely considered worthy of regard (or for cultivation) than are Macedonian or Rusyn today. Knowing that, we are becoming more aware of the ample evidence that other peoples are really concerned about their own languages too, and do not want to lose them or take them for granted. All in all, our greater interest in and concern for languages all over the world leads us directly to an awareness of the importance of literacy, in all of its varieties and individual and also societal functions. Thus, although this book focuses on the processes, problems and heroes of European vernacular literacy, it also has direct relevance for all those who are also interested in other languages and in other parts of the world. Literacy holds out great promises everywhere. Can it fulfill these promises everywhere or will it do so only partially and differentially? At any rate, like democracy (which is still far from being fully fulfilled anywhere), it is such an important human ideal and attainment that it behooves us to become better familiar with it. This book attempts to help the reader move in that direction, so that they can help move the literacy process along within their own life space.

We are about to embark on an important, interesting and at times even entertaining adventure. Our guide or vade mecum on this adventure, this book is not based upon extensive primary sources such as those that specialists employ, nor even upon extensive secondary sources that may be useful primarily to advanced students. Nevertheless, it will not only hope to supply some necessary information but also some stimulating theories, interpretations, suggestions and questions about the spread of literacy that even such students and advanced scholars may also find novel and interesting.

The type of Gutenberg's 42-line Bible (Man, 2002)

Chapter 2
What is a 'Language' of Vernacular Literacy?

Many crucial terms used in the social sciences are also used in everyday speech. The only problem is that in everyday usage terms are rarely precisely defined in advance. As a result, many a conversation that has gone on for hours may grind to a halt because one participant or another exclaims 'But that is not what I mean when *I* say "freedom" (or "democracy", or "peace", or "whatever")!' In order for us not to be faced by any such problem after many pages, or even chapters, of our discussion, let us start by immediately defining the terms 'language'. Does 'slang' qualify to be called a language? Does 'Southern English', like the kind that is spoken informally by many native residents of rural Mississippi, qualify? Does the native speech of recent Japanese immigrants from Okinawa, or that of newcomers to the US mainland from the coffee plantations near the southern coast of Puerto Rico or does the Spanish from 'South of the border, down Mexico way', qualify, because 'almost everyone's parents were native-speakers of either Spanish or one or another Amerindian language, all of which arrived here even before English did'? Does a spoken variety qualify even if it has no written counterpart at all, or even if it has no writing system? It would be good to get some of these questions clarified from the very beginning (not that full agreement may necessarily be reached even after ample discussion), so that we can all at least know if we are 'on the same page', even if we are not all on the same line of that page.

A Dictionary Definition

A commonly used unabridged dictionary suggests a typical beginning definition of language as: 'the way human beings communicate using words, whether written or spoken. It is also used for the particular system of communication used by a specific country, nation or community'

(Encarta, 1999: 1013). This particular dictionary then goes on to explain that 'language' is not the only way that individuals communicate and that it includes such subsidiary varieties as idiolects, dialects, slang, jargon, parlance, lingo, etc. The above overall definition could easily be 'filled out' by mentioning various further varieties of language, for example, occupational varieties, levels of formality in language, levels of seriousness in language, use of metaphor in language, related and unrelated languages, child language, animal languages, disturbed language, international and classical languages and so on. Gradually, what we originally took to be a simple, popular term, with a common meaning easily available to one and all, manifests itself to be full of unexpected complexities related to its widely differentiated users and uses. Obviously, only a modicum of reflection has revealed that there is nothing at all inherently simple about words such as 'language' and 'languages', since they reflect and convey all of the motivational and behavioral differences of the species that employ them, both to reveal and to disguise their goals, values and characteristics.

Indeed, the dictionary's approach quickly becomes unwieldy, as soon as we seriously try to make it apply to all of the widely known uses and users of language varieties. This type of recitation of 'varieties of varieties' also suffers from its laundry list character. There is no rhyme nor reason to the order in which we have listed them, nor any seeming relationship between these varieties, nor any attempt to cope with the obvious ephemerality and peripherality of some and the eternality and centrality of others to the human condition. There must be another way, hopefully a better one, to view language and languages, one that takes us closer to our main goal, namely, an explication of what may be a constantly ongoing saga: the birth and death of languages throughout the centuries of dramatically unequal human societies living in both internal and external interaction.

Another Approach

One of the most salient features of the manifold languages of human societies is the varying and changeable attitudes or beliefs that these societies have about them, even be they positive ones. In a very real sense, 'languages' are those whose respective speech communities want and believe them to be full-fledged verbal media in order to be able to engage in the kinds of interactions that these communities consider important for the realization of their goals. Such a definition makes us dependent on within-community attitudes in order to decide 'what is a language'. Only four such attitudinal dimensions or belief systems are required in order to generate, order and contrast a substantial 'variety of (language) varieties', as follows.

Vitality

Vitality deals with the conviction that any variety under consideration has a 'large' number of speakers, readers, writers and understanders. It forms the attitude toward languages, one's own as well as those of others, which reflects the amour propre of most speech communities (i.e. it is very perspectival in nature). In the world at large it is commonly considered more auspicious, more honorable, more noteworthy, more robust, more powerful and longevity predictive for a variety to have more speakers rather than fewer ones. However, this intuitive and commonsensical view that 'more' speakers is better than 'fewer' speakers, also flies in the face of the incontrovertible evidence that at any particular time in human history, as well as throughout human history as a whole, there have been many more numerically tiny varieties than there have been numerically 'hefty' ones. Presumably, God must have liked tiny languages, just as [s]he must have liked poor people, because [s]he made so many of them! Of course, it is also the case that there are several very persistent small languages (e.g. Basque, Letzembourgish and Montagasque, just to mention a few in tiny corners of Western Europe alone), as well as several deceased larger languages (e.g. Sumerian, Egyptian and Khazar, to mention a few Afro-Asian ones), which leads us to the realization that the brute size of a speech community per se, at one point in time, is no sure guarantee of its vitality at another.

But, all things considered, most of those who care for the health and well-being of specific languages, or for the safeguarding of a 'many-languaged-world' as a whole, easily realize that a steadily shrinking demographic base for a community of speakers tends to spell 'trouble ahead' for the speech community under discussion. Or, to put it another way, all things considered, it may be better to have the headaches of larger languages than the fevers of smaller ones. On the other hand, the advent of the computer has made small languages much more easily 'maintainable' (via websites, blogs, desktop publishing and email) and distributable (via newsletters, recipient lists and self-accessible via voluntary virtual communities) than was ever the case before, particularly since the appearance of the printing press, mass mailings, commercial advertising and massive mailing lists. But, even so, 'more' may still be better than 'less' and this leaves us with the problem of where should one draw the boundary between 'large' and 'small'? Vitality may well turn out to be another 'perspectival' issue which has no objective empirical solution; there are many such in the social sciences precisely because they so closely mirror society, even though the real world acts on the basis of intuitive understandings of where that boundary presumably lies. Varieties that are viewed as lacking vitality are more likely to die out without leaving a record, or to remain unknown to outsiders even when they are alive and intergenerationally continuous. The obvious importance of literacy functions and vitality characteristics considered together (i.e. in interaction with each other) should also not be overlooked, since either one may intensify the extent to which the other raises any variety out of perspectival invisibility. Vitality is a descriptor of languages per se while literacy is a function of languages. These two characterizations lie on two different dimensions, they are independent of each other and must be checked out independently, when investigating when and why varieties get to be recognized or utilized either by their own users or by outsiders.

Historicity

Historicity deals with the view that any given variety under discussion has a long and distinguished history. Older varieties are considered somehow 'better' than younger ones that have only just come into being. Let us define the boundary between 'older' and 'younger' as three complete generations, so that hardly anyone alive at any particular time can say that they are themselves older than a variety whose age is under discussion. Of course, a more noteworthy attribute of historicity is that it also tends to increase the opportunity that a particular variety will be associated with great writers, famous leaders and noteworthy rallying periods in its speech community's history. An even more noteworthy characteristic, for our purposes, is that historicity is widely considered to be 'a good thing' (a desirable attribute) in interlanguage comparisons and that it is commonly associated with higher prestige and greater visibility in the 'world of languages'. 'My language is older than yours is' is a claim to fame that may come in handy in struggling to maintain one's language and marshal the resources and supporters needed to protect and preserve it from a competitor variety.

Of course, any claim as to 'historicity' is a highly perspectival claim, that is, it is subjective and highly dependent on the viewer's perspective (i.e. it is self-serving in accord with and predictable from his or her prior opinions and attitudes and can only be roughly inferred from larger historical circumstances). Accurate data on the age of languages are, therefore, rare or totally absent in most cases, but the view that older is better persists nevertheless. Any estimates as to the age of one language or another must be very critically examined and considered tentative at best and socioculturally biased as a rule. Setting aside the issue of language names (most language names in current use are far younger than the languages themselves), and in some instances names have been maintained even though the languages to which they have been applied have changed two or even three times. We know that English is far younger than French, for example, because we use the dates 441–442, an estimate of when the Angles, the Saxons and the Jutes crossed the Channel from the mainland into Britain (an estimate which was already several hundred years old when it was first recorded in a document which has fortunately and accidentally survived). If true, it may then be the earliest date when a new entity, to be called 'English', could possibly have come into being. But of course, the three tribes did not immediately switch into a shared compromise variety derived from their originally different Low Germanic varieties, and when a written name first appeared for this compromise variety it was not called English at all but, rather (Old) Saxon. Old Saxon had to go through many vicissitudes of its own before the name English appeared on a manuscript. By then, or even by the date that Old Saxon came into use, the Latinate beginnings of French were, of course, well established (although, once again, the name 'French', per se, came onto the scene much later). References to Latin as the precursor language were also made for early Spanish and early Italian, just to mention two others, out of a total of six or so additional European varieties which also claimed this honor. That too, the honor of being derived from Latin, can be viewed as resulting from the allure of 'historicity' and its assumed safeguard against the presumed corruption that, it was thought, necessarily and inevitably befell all later languages.

Standardization

Proceeding with our short list of variety descriptors we come to another one that has been commonly applied to some of the world's language varieties, namely 'standardization'. No languages are born standardized, but, rather, have had standardization foisted upon them by some of their best 'friends' and greatest admirers (in order, as it were, to improve the perfect). Standardization aims at the internal 'uniformation' of any given language variety across all educated members of its speech community. It is an outgrowth or end product of an apparently later need to have a uniform spelling, an agreed upon grammar, consensual punctuation and orthoepy (pronunciation and accentuation) systems and, finally, to institute and recognize the authorities and guides that are to be recognized in order to establish and alter or revise these systems.

There is always more variation in human speech (most of it being informal and emotional) than in human writing (much of it being 'for the record', that is, for communicants not copresent when a text is being prepared) within a given speech community. As a result, written and read communications are much more likely to be precise and redundant (i.e. possessing greater length and repetitiveness) than spoken communications. Spoken communications tend to include (or try to provide for pauses) in order to imply or actually ask 'If you know what I mean?', 'Right?', 'Do you follow me?', in order to arrive at shared joint understandings (or even at joint understandings that can avoid future disagreements) that may exist between the interlocutors to a conversation. This kind of ongoing oral feedback and self-correction or repair, if recorded by a scribe and then edited by an editor, ultimately enables us to make sense of the incomplete sentences and elliptical references for which much spoken face-to-face communication is notorious and which the written record can guard against (particularly if that record itself is based upon a standardized system of notation).

Some spoken communication is not like that just mentioned at all. Consider, for example, speeches from the throne, sentence or instructions announced by judges to accuse or to juries, or religious texts and well-memorized literary recitations. These are all often quite like written texts and, indeed, may be read out from a previously prepared written text or appended to a subsequent continuing record of such texts that may accumulate over many years. Such texts 'rise above' the usual characteristics of spoken conversation between two informal parties. They are sometimes referred to as 'canned', precisely because they resemble and seek to resemble formal written material in many (or even in most) respects. That is why the variety that is intended for school-texts, 'official records' and for preservation over the ages (when neither the current speaker/writer or hearer/reader can be expected to be present for the purposes of clarification) can also be expected to be the first to be standardized with respect to writing system, orthography, grammar, punctuation and the levels of redundancy, repetition and circumlocution that prevail. Standardized varieties are least likely to enter into and to drop out of general use without any notice being taken of such events, not only insofar as the community of users is concerned, but even insofar as their neighbors are concerned.

Autonomy

The internal evaluation of varieties regarding their uniformation, on the one hand, and the external evaluation of the same varieties regarding the implications of such uniformation, on the other, are not always in agreement. Very few of the members of the native English speech community are aware of any shortcomings as to the uniformation of its spelling, and whatever awareness there may be of any such shortcomings is usually interpreted as quaint and undisturbing reminders of its historicity. From the point of view of the native French-speaking community, however, the irregularity of English spelling is certainly patent and the fact that there is no such institution as an 'Academy for the English Language', as there is for French (the Académie de la langue française presumably being the highest court of appeal regarding the correctness of French spelling or grammar), merely confirms the lawless nature of English in the eyes of many a literate French person, as it does for literate native speakers of Spanish, German, Russian, Dutch, and so on, all of whom have their own language academies. Is such a difference in perspective concerning the degree of standardization of English an embarrassment for the English? Hardly, because English certainly possesses its own 'autonomy', that is, its own perspectival certainty (developed over centuries) as to its full-fledged independence from outside control. Were this not the case, and were it not reciprocally the case, then any perspectival 'lawlessness' of English spelling would contribute to much worse judgments as to whether English was really a full-fledged and independent language at all, and might do so both internally and externally as to the speech community of native speakers of English. This latter problem is exactly the one that obtains in the case of comparisons between Frisian and Dutch, or between Macedonian and Bulgarian, or between Asturian and Spanish, or between Urdu and Hindi. But why then is 'autonomy' of such great importance in the latter cases (and many others like them), whereas it is of so little importance in the often heatedly acrimonious relationship between English and French?

'Autonomy' attains the pinnacle of crucial importance in the case of varieties that are very similar one to the other in all of their outer linguistic dimensions and yet they differ markedly in the extent to which these two languages are related to upper social power functions, for example, Dutch as related to Flemish or Ukrainian as related to Rusyn. Indeed, because of its lower 'autonomy' associations (via functions such as use in print beyond dialog, beyond poetry, beyond 'local color' regionalism, or, to put it bluntly, beyond belles-lettres more generally) due to use by governments, use as media of higher technological education, use by agencies of power such as the armed forces, some varieties get to be labeled 'dialects' instead of languages at all. As we have already noted, 'dialects' lack perspectival 'autonomy', because they are 'dialects of ...', that is, they are assigned to a lower hierarchical category than those 'above' them in the hierarchical pecking order. It is the perspectival acceptance of Spanish into the halls of power that makes it a 'real' language at the same time that Asturian is often considered to be a 'mere' dialect, even by many of its own speakers, notwithstanding its marked similarity to Castilian (or, precisely because of its marked similarity to Castilian).

Will the ultimate completion of the long awaited and eagerly expected unabridged dictionary of Frisian finally secure that variety's perspectival 'autonomy' vis-à-vis Dutch? 'Not likely', insofar as native speakers (and readers or writers) of Netherlandish are concerned. A great dictionary is a sign of standardization, but it is still far short of representing a recognized claim to the vital control over an 'army and a navy' that 'autonomy' specifies. 'Standardization' is a consensual intragroup judgment as to the ability of the internal arbiters of a variety's variability to insist upon and to succeed at its acceptance for formal functions. Finally, moreover, 'autonomy' is a consensual intergroup judgment as to a variety's intragroup acceptance for its most important formal functions.

When viewed from a worldwide perspective, 'autonomy' represents a higher status of completion and/or perfection, precisely because it represents the ability of variety B's internal arbiters of correctness and wielders of power to obtain the approval of variety A's corresponding arbiters as to B's freedom from foreign control or influence in setting up its own standardization criteria. Only a variety with 'sufficient' access to power of its own can attain such reciprocal recognition of unblemished language stature as the attribution of 'autonomy' implies. This is doubly the case if B is structurally very similar to A and it is triply the case if B is noticeably weaker (i.e. less power-related) than is A, even if in its own bailiwick it is used for all formal functions. 'Beauty is in the eye of the beholder' and it is the 'outside beholder' that counts since the self-attribution of beauty represents only a weak claim in that connection. So too it is with 'autonomy'. A powerful outsider's vote of confidence in a variety's 'autonomy' is more crucial by far in fighting off the invidious 'dialect' charge than is an insider's (particularly if the insider's vote does little to attain greater access to formal usage, i.e. to power usage) for the speech community. This is vital insofar as mutual literacy recognition is concerned as well.

The concordance between two perspectival continua

Varieties with the most protected formal or reading/writing functions and the most firmly instituted governmental or religious functions are also the same ones that are likely to be regarded as autonomous. These are also the varieties that are least changeable and least forgettable. They are least likely to be lost, to die out or to drop out of usage even when no longer widely spoken (or to suddenly come into highly honorific usage and poser-charged functions) without serious dislocations related to the kinds of widespread social change that are likely to reach the record-books of local scribes. Conversely, those varieties that have never attained any formal functions are least likely to be noticed when born or visibly missed when gone. Thus, one conclusion that can be arrived at about the recent increases in numbers of dying languages (and the recent increases – although less dramatically so – in the numbers of newly elevated languages of literacy) has to do with the spread of literacy from social class to social class or from one polity to another.

The functions attained by languages that have been newly 'clocked in' and the functions surrendered by those declared to be 'out and over with', are all social change related. Such changes do not occur – not even changes in the records per se (as distinct from changes in actual language use in society) – without social dislocation. We are no longer living in an age when languages 'go softly into the night', not even when they are at the lower end of the social power and status distributions. The communication media that blanket the world – particularly in English and in conjunction with the spread of English (speak of social power and social change!) – have changed our record keeping and record posting as well. Even so, we are probably unaware of more of the 'losers' than of the 'winners'. We must try to correct for this disparity in consciousness, particularly since we anglophones ourselves are more likely to be in the circle of the winners, whether by ethnic identity, mother tongue, social class and/or professional orientation. As spreaders of literacy in general and of English literacy in particular, we are naturally disinclined to see ourselves as implicated in the language deaths that we abhor, but implicated we are, whether we abhor them or not. We must all acknowledge our co-complicity if 'language justice' is ever to be attained.

We have touched upon several topics in trying to answer the seemingly simple question 'what is a language?' We need to answer the latter question if we are ever to reliably answer such subsequent and more difficult ones as 'how many languages are dying and how can we describe them in sociofunctional terms?', 'is the number of language deaths larger than it was before?' and 'is their death-rate greater than their birth-rate?' However, by keeping in mind the questions about language death and language birth that many of those concerned with literacy may ultimately want to answer, we have come to an early and quite unexpected realization that there are various kinds ('varieties') of languages and that these varieties differ greatly from one another not only demographically (size, age distribution) but also sociofunctionally, perspectivally and in terms of the cultural roles that are acknowledged for them.

Those varieties that are involved in literacy functions (or in major, formal, spoken ceremonies) are also more likely to be dignified as 'languages' and, accordingly, their appearance and disappearance are more likely to draw attention upon themselves, to become matters of record (and therefore remembered over a much longer expanse of time) and to be assigned caretakers and gatekeepers. It is only comparatively lately that the varieties of small and nonliterate populations have entered into our field of vision and that their increasing involvements in literacy (basic folk-schooling), secondary and postsecondary education, religious services and governmental activity and actions, has alerted us to the fact that our records at this end of the distribution of varieties are much better than those at the end characterized by informality, oralcy and face-to-face interaction alone. The latter phenomenon is a by-product of both econotechnical and of sociocultural change, changes which also are involved in the continued promotion of such varieties into high-end functions that have hitherto been entirely closed to them. Thus, although we cannot expect to overcome entirely the perspectival biases downwards and upwards of which we are aware, we can attempt to counter or correct them somewhat by counter-perspectival corrections of our own, modulated by whatever information and insight we can bring to bear on the issue.

As more and more investigators become seriously interested in examining questions such as these and, therefore, in examining the literature that such interests generate, the more there will be a variety of estimates of literacy, each maintained by whatever goals, data and interpretations of each such examination reveals. We remain hopeful that our examinations will yield more understanding in the long run, because they can inform and be of help at least to some, in the short term.

Scalability: Attributes That Presuppose Others

It may not seem obvious at first blush, but the property that characterizes each 'step' in a progression from one type of variety to another (e.g. 'the attribute of being involved in literacy instruction') may itself be 'predictable', 'scalable' or 'reproducible' from other attributes that are also utilized for this purpose. This is so if a rank-order progression exists between these 'attributes' such that the attribute that exists to the 'highest' (rarest, most difficult, most advanced, etc.) degree among them in positing step 5, for example, also exists to a slightly lesser degree in step 4, while those of step 4 also pertain to step 3, those of step 3 also pertain to step 2 and those of step 2 also pertain in this way to those of step 1. If a further step, step 6, is subsequently identified, then, for it to be a member of a scalable series, it must be such that except for its own newly discovered highest step it is entirely found within the steps below it. The specific nature of the highest point at any step defines that step and there is simply no other way in which to reach that step other than via the addition and inclusion of that particular step and all that preceded it.

Not many properties of social behavior are scalable, but age is, income is, generational membership since the arrival of immigrants in the United States from country X is, etc. All that scalability requires, actually, is that there be few (optimally, 'no') 'ties' in the rankings of attributes within any set of attributes being scored, and as much agreement as possible (optimally, full agreement) among the rankers of each individual attribute. Does this sound pretty theoretical and confusing? An example will clarify this quickly. Assume, as in Table 2.1, that we have a group of n judges such that we can ask them each to judge, on a +/− basis, a number of varieties with which they are all well acquainted, as to which (if any) of the below-mentioned attributes are appropriate descriptors of the varieties

Table 2.1 Example of a highly reproducible scale

	Attributes			
Varieties	Vitality[a]	Historicity[b]	Autonomy[c]	Standardization[d]
Literary	X	X	X	X
Vernacular	X	X	X	
Dialect	X	X		
Creole	X			
Pidgin				
Classical		X	X	X
IAL[e]			X	X
Code				X

[a]Vitality = The attribute of being judged to have many mother-tongue speakers.
[b]Historicity = The attribute of being older than any one currently alive.
[c]Autonomy = The attribute of establishing its own *internally* recognized rules.
[d]Standardization = The attribute of establishing its own *externally* recognized rules.
[e]International Auxiliary Language, for example, Esperanto.

in question. If, upon analysis of the judgments obtained, one variety is consensually judged to have only Vitality; the second also has Historicity, the third also Standardization and the fourth also Autonomy, then Table 2.1 is obtained. (We will pause to define each of these attributes after reviewing the table.)

Once we have consensually defined the above four attributes, their patterned distributions (both their distinctive absences and presences) defines eight different varieties. The varieties that are judged to possess Standardization and Autonomy (literary and classical) will interest us most from here on, since they are the only ones that are then readily recognized for the purposes of vernacular and classical literacy. The road to such recognition first travels through the hinterlands of being recognized for Vitality and Historicity. The road that must be traveled before such consensual recognition is obtained is often a long, difficult and conflicted one, whether it is the struggle of some for their dialect to be consensually considered as a full-fledged vernacular with standardization of its own, or the struggle of these same vernaculars later to be consensually recognized as being autonomous and unconstrained by the standards of their erstwhile 'betters'. The progression from pidgin to creole is more a natural biological one (the birth of a generation for whom the former makeshift pidgin is now a normal and omnipresent mother-tongue with the innovative linguistic expansion and internal functional diversification) that may then become possible. Every change in scalability position involves a struggle of some kind. The consensual attainment of classical status is certainly not uneventful. It requires not only the passage of at least three generations of language maintenance without mother-tongue speakers (there are literally thousands of varieties that would qualify on this basis alone), but of passing beyond the stage of various negative judgments (with which our table does *not* attempt to deal) to successfully pursue the acquisition of honorific status based on the historical record primarily based on literacy and the extant written (printed, read and/or recited) works of former days, centuries and millennia.

Languages of regional classical literacy are often the predecessors of one or more local languages of literacy. IAL status (International Auxiliary Language) may also subsume an aspiration among some of its users to attain vitality (i.e. to pass the variety on to their children as a mother tongue rather than only as a variety acquired subsequently) and when that happens (as it has, e.g. among small groups of Esperantists) a new vernacular may be said to come into being. The same progression is only theoretically possible for code varieties, since a basic feature of codes is the fact that they are hidden and even secret and, therefore, they are far from being likely to be passed on in the usual ('natural') intergenerational fashion, which is at least a partial desideratum for IALs.

The unique and complete scalability of the above distinctive combinations and permutations of varieties and their attributes is an indication of how complex and yet how systematically efficient the theoretical definitions of language varieties can be. Such systematic formality (which actually amounts to greater simplicity) is characteristic of scientific approaches to phenomena that may have long been popularly but unsystematically observed before. Only one variety pertains to an empty set: pidgin, defined in Table 2.1 by its complete lack on every attributable front. The distinct benefit of this type of formal derivation of varietal definitions is that each attribute can either be combined or considered separately for the purposes of complete data examination. There is, therefore, no advance or cut and dry answer to our beginning question. We must first agree on matters such as the above (the absence and presence of a specified set of attributes and the varieties generated by them), if we are ever to be able to agree on what is a language, why new varieties are ever born and why old ones ever die out, serve different purposes (one among them being 'literacy'), gratify different passions and facilitate different missions – including many not foreseen or even foreseeable at any given moment in time. Settle back for a magnificent journey! There may very well be no 'final word' in this discussion; the ultimate wisdom is not to say the last word, but to keep looking for new and differently patterned ways in which sentient beings and their societies go about communicating (and also mis-communicating) 'what's (supposedly) on their minds'.

Whether or not our minds and our varieties are scalable in some sort of related fashion ('the jury is still out on that'), the varieties and the attributes of varieties considered above (Table 2.1), will be utilized time and again in the chapters that follow in our pursuit of a systematic understanding of the rise and development of European languages of vernacular literacy.

Working with estimates of the prevalence of vernacular literacy when past generations are the focus of inquiry

Since this book seeks to focus on the spread of European vernacular literacy, we must agree on whether and to what degree such literacy has arrived at any given time and place. Several international definitions of adult literacy have been accepted during the past century, but these definitions do not begin to solve the problems of investigating 'differentials in the rise of literacy' that can serve us retroactively. One of the widely adopted definitions of literacy that is used today is 'the ability to read and write...at levels of proficiency necessary to function on the job and to achieve one's goals and develop one's knowledge and potential...The National American Literacy Survey (NALS) has determined that level of education has the strongest relationship to demonstrated literacy proficiency...Education's goal must be to assist every individual to possess the level of skills needed to keep pace with the rising demands in today's society. Today, lifelong learning needs to become a way of life. As levels of education rise, so will the minimum level required for functional adult literacy. This level has risen from 4th grade to 8th grade to 12th grade level, from the time of the First World War to the beginning of the 21st century.'

Even if we were to attempt to apply the basic features of the above definition to all parts of Europe today, the requisite comparable data are just not available, not even if we simply use a measure of ability to read a simple running text of modest length. This is ever so much more the case if we attempt to study the rise of European vernacular literacy over time, for example, since the days of Gutenberg. Accordingly, we will just have to do the best we can, attempting to improve the reliability and the validity of our estimates over the long range. Neither the substantive nor the methodological problems that we have just acknowledged are destined for early resolution on a comparative contemporary basis, much less so on the retroactive one. Nevertheless, as we will soon see in the chapters that follow, enough progress has been made in that connection in order to arrive at meaningful estimates in that direction.

Chapter 3
The Rise of Vernaculars of Literacy in Europe

The major context in which it might be easiest to begin an exploration of the arrival of popular (i.e. folk, not elitist) literacy is in Europe. This is the continent where (1) this phenomenon and related topics have been documented most thoroughly, and (2) where the concern for language use in social contexts has been greatest, not only among clergy, scholars and nobility but, also, among entrepreneurs in trade, commerce and industry, as well as increasingly among city folk in the more educated as well as in working classes and beyond. It could very well be that the prevalence of such concerns, and the data collection to which they lead, may either directly or subtly influence the results of our inquiry. However, there is no place in the world where particular local circumstances are not copresent and where their investigation will not influence the outcomes under study, and so they should. So we may as well begin our search where there is enough suggestive data to stimulate our thinking, keeping in mind that it is not magnitudes that really interest us fundamentally but, rather, the social processes that underlie them. We are more interested in where, when and why new vernacular literacies arise, than in how large and influential are the numbers of their associated clienteles.

Introducing Karl W. Deutsch (1912–1992) and Time 1 (T1)

Fortunate indeed are those who can stand on the shoulders of giants, because thanks to these giants those who come later can often see further than could even their illustrious predecessors. The famous (Czech-) American scholar, Karl W. Deutsch, one of the most innovative and productive fathers of the modern study of national communication, both in the macro- and in the micro-political arenas, is the giant who provides us with shoulders that are broader and taller than most of his (or even of our own) contemporaries. His classic *Nationalism and Social Communication* (1953; rev. 1966, and originally based upon his 1951 dissertation) is a good place to become acquainted, or to renew one's past acquaintance, with him for all those under the mistaken assumption that any work essentially over half a century old must be entirely an outdated one by now. Indeed, many of the nuggets in classic works that are all too often passed by today are well worth (re-) investigating.

In the early years of World War II, Deutsch undertook to trace the course of literacy in Europe during the past millennium. He estimated, on the basis of a careful review of sources preserved and published in a large variety of archival and library sources, that in the year 950 C.E. (later referred to as R1 in our tables, below) there were only six languages of literacy on that entire continent, namely, Latin, Greek, Hebrew, Old Church Slavonic (Old Bulgarian), Arabic and Anglo-Saxon. Two observations are in order here: (1) In connections with this subset of languages there is little problem as to 'what do we mean by literacy or how widespread it was'. All of these languages are by now (and were even then) 'classicals' and, as such, literacy via them was largely limited to the clergy and was, therefore, of varied fluency and frequency but tended to be ritualized in any case; (2) this is a startlingly nonrandom list, vis-à-vis all the languages then existing in Europe, precisely because of the classical religious texts with which all but the last one were and still are associated to this present day, over 1100 years later. Even the last-mentioned of these, Anglo-Saxon, was closely associated with the chronicles (e.g. *Beowulf*) and the accounts of the Church fathers. In a time and place where vernacular translation of Holy Scripture was either condemned or simply undreamed of, Anglo-Saxon tales too were a means of spreading the faith and fostering education among the laity, in a variety closer to, but soon (or even *ab initio*), not identical with any of the other Germanic vernaculars of the south of England. It is here that our examination of vernacular literacy begins.

Thus, inauspiciously, we have added a very vital two-step flow to our previous one-step emphasis on classical literacy alone, to literacy that went a little beyond the male clergy (plus a few favored members of the laity), and slowly, very slowly initially, and surely, reached 'even beyond' the all male laity. We may safely assume that many, many vernaculars also existed in Europe in those early T1-times and that sociocultural values and changes often required one sort or another of accommodation with them even in speech, either via vernacular bilingualism (but not yet via vernacular biliteracy) or via pagan or syncretistic religious varieties that were related to (or predecessors of) the Abrahamic ones and their respective vernaculars. It may also be that Karl W. Deutsch overlooked a few other early European carriers of literacy (at least one Celtic variety was probably current among their clergy even then, and a Viking or Norse one, and a mid-Germanic one, and perhaps a few others of roughly similarly restricted elitistic literacy), some of which may have fallen between the 'cracks' of his nonoverlapping time intervals; however, let us remain with his account as a starting point.

Deutsch throws no light on the then-concurrent spoken languages of that time (much less, light on even earlier ones), nor on the means by which any of these or other restricted literacies that may have existed were safeguarded, propagated and cultivated, either with or 'without the benefit of clergy'. Conquest by the sword, location on trade routes, expulsions, immigrations and pilgrimages, the spread of religions and the wanderings of their spokespersons, governmental operations and tax collections, wandering bards and minstrels, folk celebrations that often dated back to pre-Christian days, the simultaneous growth of private enterprises and public administration, all must be taken into account to explain why literacy appeared precisely in a few places where records of it have fortunately (and sometimes almost accidentally) been preserved against the ravages of time, fire, water, warfare and 'other acts of God'.

Then as now, the number of actively spoken vernacular varieties and the variety of carriers of literacy initially differed greatly, even if related, with the former providing a seemingly inexhaustible pool out of which the latter could ultimately be formed and re-formed (not only in the near range, but in the further and still unfathomed range as well). The local stories and influences may (and do) differ in detail but they all revolve around the complex interactions between the mega-factor ultimately renamed socialcultural change, which subsumes social class differentiations as well. Nevertheless, most of the roughly 'big six literary classicals of Europe' have retained much of their aura and distinction from that day to this, and almost all of them have even retained a residual nonvernacular literacy function to this very day. But a time of significant change was nigh (see Table 3.1, based upon Deutsch's 1966 discussion, but of our own construction).

Time 2 (T2): 1250 C.E. and the Next Few Centuries Thereafter[1]

Deutsch skips 300 years, to 1250, for his second stocktaking of languages of literacy in Europe. It is in this period that we find the beginnings of popular vernacular literacy in Europe. Deutsch reports that during this time period, only one language, Provençal, apparently both entered and

Table 3.1 Vernaculars of Literacy in Europe: 950–1990[a]

	950:T1	1250:T2	1800:T3	1900:T4	1937:T5	1990:T6
Classicals						
Hebrew	x	x	x	x[b]	x[b]	x[b]
Greek	x	x	x	x[b]	x[b]	x[b]
Latin	x	x	x	x	x	x
Arabic	x	x	x	x	x[b]	x[b]
Slavonic (Old Bulg)	x	x	x	–	–	–
Anglo-Saxon	x	–	–	–	–	–
Romance						
French	–	x	x	x	x	x
Spanish	–	x	x	x	x	x
Portuguese	–	x	x	x	x	x
Italian	–	x	x	x	x	x
Catalan	–	x	c	x	x	x
Provençal	–	x	c	–	–	–
Roumanian	–	–	–	x	x	x
Scandinavian						
Icelandic	–	x	x	x	x	x
Danish	–	x	x	x	x	x
Swedish	–	x	x	x	x	x
Norwegian/Ryks	–	x	x	x	x	x
Landsmaal/Ninorsk	–	–	–	–	x	x
Other Germanic						
English	–	–	x	x	x	x
Hi-German	–	–	x	–	–	–
Lo-German	–	–	x	x	–	–
German	–	–	–	x	x	x

(Continued)

Table 3.1 Continued

	950:T1	1250:T2	1800:T3	1900:T4	1937:T5	1990:T6
Dutch	–	–	x	x	x	x
Yiddish	–	–	c	x	x	x
Flemish	–	–	–	x	x	d
Slavic						
Russian	–	x	x	x	x	x
Polish	–	–	x	x	x	x
Czech	–	–	–	x	x	x
Slovak	–	–	–	x	x	x
Serbo-Croatian	–	–	–	x	x	x
Slovene	–	–	–	x	x	x
Bulgarian	–	–	–	x	x	x
Ukrainian	–	–	–	x	x	x
Other						
Hungarian (Magyar)	–	–	x	x	x	x
Turkish (Osmanli)	–	–	x	x	x	x
Finnish	–	–	–	x	x	x
Estonian/Lith/Latv	–	–	–	x	x	x
European USSR	–	–	–	–	13[e]	13[e]
Other European	–	–	–	–	7[f]	7[f]
Totals	6	16	24	32	52	51

[a]This table is derived from Deutsch 1942, with additions and corrections as noted in the footnotes that follow. The data for 1990 are derived from Heinz Kloss and Grant D. McConnell, Linguistic Composition of the Nations of the World, University of Laval Press, 1974–1984.
[b]Both the classical and modernized varieties are used in print.
[c]Deutsch provides no precise indications for this year, although the language was probably used in print in this T-period.
[d]Flemish and Dutch are now considered as two spoken varieties of one and the same written variety.
[e]Underestimate: The 1990 indications are from Kloss and McConnell (1974–1984) and includes Byelorussian, Karelian, and so on.
[f]Underestimate: The 1990 indications are from Kloss and McConnell, op. cit., and includes Irish, Scots, Welsh, *et al.*

departed from the ranks of such literacy during the 300 years of its duration. Another, Anglo-Saxon, was 'submerged', never to reappear as such. The other six literacies of 950 (i.e. T1) continued to function as such and were joined by 11 newcomers: High German ('High' refers to the southern mountain area of Germany, rather than to any cultural superiority), Low German (in the northern lowlands of the region), French, Icelandic, Russian, Spanish, Catalan, Portuguese, Italian, Swedish and Norwegian. With respect to this list, Deutsch quotes an earlier scholar, G. Sarton (v.1:1927–v.2:1931) to the effect that 'deeper study would [also] introduce other languages; I speak [here] only of those ... [of] exceptional vitality or ... [fostered] by the creation of masterpieces' (v. 2.: 293). 'Vitality', in Sarton's sense, refers only to comparatively rapid and plentiful population growth, which may have displaced certain neighboring vernacular varieties (at least insofar as becoming maximally useful bearers of literacy was concerned, rather than in the narrower attitudinal sense in which we have encountered it earlier in Chapter 2). 'The creation of (literary) masterpieces', however, is another kind of variable. It is necessarily more directly linked, even if not completely so, to a spoken (and therefore natively understood) variety among the nonclerical population, that is, to a particular kind of new consumer: the urban and more urbane denizen. As city populations increased, as they certainly did, slowly but steadily, during the 300-year period between T1 and T2, a class of owners of properties and of businesses appeared that had its own educational, occupational and amusement interests and needs. Mastery of the classical languages of literacy required more time, ability and effort than most of this class were able to devote to their pursuit, and more engagement with religious texts, many of which provided neither the enjoyment nor the skills and profits expected by most of these newly reachable readers. Thus it was that vernaculars made their first appearances at the front doors of European literacy. If we look for them before T2, we either cannot find them at all or find only peripheral shreds of evidence of their presence, but clearly that does not mean that they did not exist at all. Nor does their appearance 'on the record' in T2 (see Table 3.1), indicate any sudden *ex nihilo* creation. Indeed, they had all existed before T2, although not necessarily under their current names. Thus far, they had been 'merely oral vernaculars' and, therefore, they usually left no written records by means of which to document their arrival, existence and, in all but the most fortunate cases, not even the length of their persistence at all. In many instances they were probably similar in functions to many of the recently disappearing vernaculars of our own day. Even for those that survived, whose pamphlets or chapbooks triumphed over floods, fires and other calamities, or were mentioned in church or other records, we have no evidence as to how many readers they had or of how well they could read. These questions arise throughout Deutsch's table, of course, and they sometimes remain to this very day in more recent regional studies of literacy.

Even more significant than the 'disappearance' or eclipse of Anglo-Saxon in T2 (just where it could have 'gone to', and why, will be commented upon in Chapter 4) is the 'appearance' of several Romance vernaculars of literacy (five to be exact: French, Spanish, Catalan, Portuguese and Italian), four Scandinavian ones (Norwegian, Swedish, Danish and Icelandic), three other Germanic ones (Dutch, High German and Low German) and one Slavic vernacular (Russian). Thus, all of the European classicals have been retained in Europe from T1 to T2. The vehicles of church usage alter slowly, not only because church-associated and sanctioned texts themselves usually do not change much or rapidly. Even if they 'ever' change at all, the vehicles of these texts have little immediate relevance for the out-of-church lives of their newly literate urban readers, and, conversely, the texts are therefore little impacted by then-modern urban life. This out-of-sync tendency finally results in noticeable change in the varieties utilized for a more secular vernacular literacy relative to its religious predecessor.

By adding at least as many as five vernaculars from the various branches of the Germanic language family, including English, all major branches of Germanic come to be represented by the time T2 terminates and T3 begins. Accordingly, the Germanic family became one of the earliest to attain full representation in the 'European literacy club', even before the Middle Ages ended. These intrafamilial vernaculars differ from each other on a geographic basis, thereby destroying the parsimony that had long been provided by both the classicals and the semipetrified quasi-religious vernaculars, choosing instead to travel the long path of later local cultural autonomy and, ultimately, political separation that a vernacular that is more truly considered to be 'one's own' makes possible.

Where did these new vernaculars in T2 come from? They all probably existed in T1 but had grown further apart during their own separate vernacular development, to the point that they were no longer as mutually understandable as they may well have been 'originally'. 'Variety is the spice of life', it is said, and, indeed, it is present in all living things, certainly including vernacular varieties, and most particularly in those that are spread over greater expanses. In all of the latter, the absence of roads, the rarity of face-to-face interaction with their broader families of origin and their differing degrees and kinds of interaction with 'kinfolk' who become distant, no matter how related they may have once been at the level of historic memories or imaginations, resulted in ever greater communication gaps both in reality and in possibility.

All of the foregoing trends tend to foster societal differentiation, precisely because they curtail communication to and from 'remoter' population centers each with their own typical realia (specific kinds of animal life, specific kinds of foods, specific kinds of indigenous cultures encountered and submerged, specific natural resources and topography, etc.), all of which engender discontinuities in the interests and concerns that fashion the very cores of vernacular varieties. Of course, certain regional differences may already have existed between the varieties involved at their various times of departure from their original core settlements, thereby yielding $x1$, $x2$, $x3$ ... xn spoken versions from the very outset (or from even before the very outset) of their resettlement and subsequent vernacular literacy attainment.

This same scenario that applied to the differences between the vernacular 'Latins' established on foreign soil by legions departing from Rome in *different* centuries and rotating from one provincial part of the Empire to another, also applied to the resulting vernaculars themselves during T2. Many of these differences continued and impacted the resulting vernaculars, which got to be known under their own local or regional names. Although the Roman commanders may have read roughly the same kind of Latin, neither these commanders nor their legionnaires spoke identically the same kinds of Latin vernaculars. They had departed for vastly different parts of that far-flung Empire over a period of centuries. This process of further differentiation between what were then already somewhat two greatly different kinds of vernacular Latins, was then repeated and compounded over subsequent centuries. The speakers of Xish varieties of former-Latins and of Latin-impacted vernaculars from within the former Roman Empire, successively resettled in newly occupied points $x1$, $x2$, $x3$ ... xn. All of which is tantamount to saying that those (Romanic, Germanic, etc.) vernaculars that were already different instruments of literacy in T2 must not be assumed to ever having been identical vernaculars. Indeed, we will encounter these several processes of further local differentiation of hitherto apparently unified classicals or other already more or less varied varieties, first in connection with the resulting vernaculars and then, quite predictably, for diffentiated vernacular literacies too. T2 is not only a time of expansion in the number of vernaculars of literacy, but also in their own diversification and divergence, above all in power with respect to the control of scarce commodities. Since there were few schools and little formal schooling for the bulk of the population, literacy must have spread by self-mastery, informal tutelage and on-the-job-training.

The Rise of Vernaculars of Literacy in Europe   27

The work of Shakespeare began to appear and spread during this period, although Deutsch's table does not mention English explicitly until T3.

Time 3 (T3): 1800 C.E.

Let us leave for later (Chapter 5 'Heroes') the issue of the possible role of great works of literature in the birth and diffusion of vernacular literacies, since we must also consider the possibility that such works may also well have *required* more literacy than they stimulated. We will return to that topic and also to the topic of T1 varieties missing from the T2 list. Now, instead of continually shifting our attention between new arrivals and new departures from the Deutsch list, we will remain in the 'new arrivals' mode until the end of this chapter and begin here the examination of Deutsch's list for *c.*1800. We can note that among the classical, all but Anglo-Saxon again remain in use, even though it needs to be stressed that Hebrew, Greek and even Arabic have also begun their modernizations, whether on a literacy or on a vernacular basis, or both. In their cases some written forms begin to be cultivated, such that in its own respective setting some varieties of literacy and of oralcy began to approximate one another more closely. These are examples of the relatively rare phenomenon re-vernacularizations of the classicals, leading to vernacular literacies alongside of the classical literacies that had preceded them. Among the vernaculars of literacy in T3 we still find the big four Romance tongues (French, Spanish, Portuguese and Italian), but Catalan and particularly Provençal are by then apparently less related to literacy than heretofore (although in the Catalan case, if this was indeed so, it was only temporarily so). Literacies in three Scandinavian vernaculars are still present (Icelandic, Swedish and Danish) and Norwegian puts in its first appearance, but still as a variety of Danish (Dano-Norwegian, later Ryksmal). For the first time five new Germanic languages appear on the list (English, Lo- and Hi-German, Dutch and, for the first time, Yiddish), as do two Slavic tongues (Russian and, for the first time, Polish) and two newcomers originally of Asian provenience, Hungarian (Magyar) and Turkish (Osmanli), and later at least four more. Thus, by T3 we have 25 European languages of literacy in 1899 (10 more than by 1250), and, once again, there are no losses, while the earlier loss of Anglo-Saxon has again not been (and never will be) made up. Nevertheless, it is still odd that English apparently arrives so late, so to speak, even later than Russian, a quirk resulting from the name change between English and its predecessor Anglo-Saxon and the 'over-length' of the hiatus between T2 and T3 relative to the other inter-T hiatuses.

Time 4 (T4): 1900

The period of elapsed time from T1 to T3 is approximately a millennium, whereas that which elapsed from T3 to T4 is only a century. Nevertheless, the rate of increase during each of these two time periods is disproportionately in favor of the second and much briefer of the two. Whereas a gain of 19 varieties of literacy occurred in the first millennium which Deutsch has covered, there was a gain of 'only' seven in the century between T3 and T4. For our analytic purposes it is highly regrettable that the T2–T3 interval is so much longer than any coming either before or after it, thus partially hiding from view the true progression through the centuries of growth of languages of literacy. Nevertheless, if every century after 950 had reported only the same gain as that which occurred between 1800 and 1900, then there would have been not merely 25 vernaculars of literacy in Europe by 1800 but well over a hundred! Obviously, something quite different must have transpired in Western Europe first between the 13th and the 18th century (to slow the rate of growth down) and, then again, between the 18th and 19th century (to speed the rate of growth up), particularly in the Slavic (and secondarily in the 'Other') sections thereof. Furthermore, the varieties associated with literacy have become much more dispersed throughout the length and breadth of Europe in the later time period. Nevertheless, the half millennium between 1250 and 1800 witnessed a remarkable increase in both the 'other Germanic' vernaculars of literacy as well as in the noteworthy appearance of non-Indo-European vernacular literacies previously almost entirely unrepresented on the European continent. Furthermore, by the time we reach the 20th century, that is, by the year 1900 (= T4), both of the foregoing processes have continued their truly remarkable expansion to the virtual maximum possible for them.

Obviously, the growth in number and in diversity of European carriers of vernacular literacy during the 650 years between 950 and 1900 must be indicative of other societal and economic differentiations that transpired at roughly the same time. What might these have been? We will return to this question upon completing our review of Table 3.1.

Times 5 and 6 (T5 and T6) (1937 and 1990)

It is not easy to keep in mind all of the details presented in Table 3.1 for the first four 'times' reviewed thus far. But it is also not necessary to retain all of them for our general and introductory purposes. What is desirable is to reach an understanding of the kinds of societal changes that underlie the growth in vernaculars of literacy that we have already commented upon in passing and that we will now continue to trace to the end of the 20th century. T5 witnesses the arrival into the 'halls of literacy' of many of the smaller, often minoritized and post-World War I 'liberated' minority languages of Eastern Europe (Karelian, Byelorussian, Moldavian, Georgian, Ossetian, Bashkir, Cheremise, Chuvash, Mordvin, Samoyed, Komi, Tartar and Votiak) and also languages of smaller and often minoritized local significance that were previously bypassed in Western and Central Europe (Irish, Scottish Gaelic, Welsh, Basque, Breton, Romansh, Sorbian and Albanian). Interestingly enough, no further expansion along these lines can be noted from Deutsch's sources regarding Europe after World War II (although substantial further growth did occur in vernacular literacy on all other continents during that period). The war itself was probably instrumental in lifting many of the languages that are subsequently listed for the first time across the level of literacy by T5. Both war experiences and ideologically inspired literacy movements (capitalist-democratic and communist) required intensified communication with previously ignored groups and ended with institutions and media for literacy in their vernaculars. These could no longer be easily rescinded or countermanded thereafter in a world in which everyone was listening and watching. European vernacular literacy began to change from being an aspect of national into being an aspect of international attention.

Modern wars are mobilizational experiences that leave a lasting impact on the populations that survive them. Wars often move populations from rural to urban residences, where resources can more effectively reach them and where communications via vernaculars of literacy play more decisive roles, particularly in a period when the nonprint media do not yet function widely and where urban agitation for literacy can be presented as a patriotic duty with manifold personal and collective benefits. In the absence of holocausts, wars sadly add to literacy among citizen-soldiers, both on the home front and along the line of fire. Europe has contributed much to life the world over, the pleasures and advantages of literacy being first and foremost among them, as well as to the agonies of literacy, to which Europe has also contributed much more than its fair share. As with so much of modern life, popular literacy has not been an unmixed blessing by any means. The lists of the war-dead, of the maimed, the gassed and the cremated were all prepared by (and not infrequently abetted by) populations that were vernacularly literate and often highly so. The dawn and triumph of vernacular literacy unfortunately did not (as had been hoped) usher in a new era of kindness and decency between human beings.

It is enough that it raised the average level of literacy, both in Europe and elsewhere.

Toward Understanding Some of the Essential Society-wide Characteristics of Literacy

Let us now pause briefly to review the societal antecedents of the coming into being of literacy-related vernaculars. And let us preface this discussion by asking 'What can the social sciences predict'? Are the social sciences really sciences like 'the real sciences', the natural sciences, that is, can they test hypotheses, make, confirm or disconfirm predictions, or are they (as some social scientists jokingly say to one another) only able to 'predict the past'. From my point of view, predicting the past is not a little matter or a trivial intellectual or potentially useless pursuit. To better understand the past (a goal of the study of history, literature, philosophy and various sociodisciplines [including sociolinguistics and social planning as well]) is something that the creative mind cannot engage in too much. I would be proud indeed to be accused of attempting to do so, let alone of having done so successfully at least to some small extent. Having constrained myself to the confining limits of an 'introductory introduction', I cannot hope for earth-shattering innovations and fundamental proofs here, but perhaps there are some interesting tidbits and some worthwhile things that have not exactly been said before.

'Vivifying' the dead; 'freezing' the lively

Literacy involves a transformation of language in use. From the oral–aural medium which was present from its birth onward (with all of its spontaneity, informality, idiosyncracies and frequent codependence on facial and bodily reinforcement), literacy fostered a new dependence on unseen, unheard and even unknown interlocutors and, thereby, forged a new and greater need for redundancy in order to recoup via a stress on accuracy some of what had been lost in terms of physical and emotional eye-to-eye immediacy. In the realm of literacy, the laws of grammar and formality are more usually in force and sentences appeared as basic units of analysis and composition. To the extent that literacy has often carried the imprimature of 'revealed' intercultural languages, they correspondingly frequently lost in uniqueness as well as in spontaneity, often more than they immediately gained in felt power vis-à-vis rememberability, preservability and political effectiveness. Literacy turned all but the most effective first language interlocutors into second-language-like orators and actors whose spelling pronunciations were more often taken as cultured refinements rather than as the laughable pomposity and hypercorrections that only a reciprocal ignorance could ignore. For all its service as an aide-memoire, literacy often served to mystify and confuse more than to enlighten and edify, before it became the common good of the middle and upper classes. There are still huge segments of the population for whom that is the case (or very nearly the case) even today, precisely because the democratization of reading and writing has been greatly increased, albeit very far from fully realized.

In most cultures of literacy, literacy inculcation takes an inordinate amount of learning time, even among pupils whose own mother tongue is involved (a hallmark of T4) while taking a great deal away from the achievement of anywhere near the degree of pleasure, stimulation and edification that good literature could provide, because of the time consumed by instruction in reading, writing and grammar. The largely empty and formal flourishes of literacy often triumphed over communication per se. English certainly became a language of literacy many centuries ago, but, by and large, English in print has often become a school-learned language of illiteracy for most learners in most parts of the world (including many in the English mother-tongue parts thereof as well). This is not to gainsay the roles of schools and teachers in this entire process, but requisite vernacular literacy has always been a product of so much more than schools and formal education. The immensity of the total process of 'literarization' can begin to be appreciated by turning first to a consideration which is often overlooked: the introduction of literacy into Europe varies significantly with the points of the compass (i.e. with other phenomena that can initially be grasped if they are initially suggested along geographic lines).

The spatial dimension of literacy: The West to East and the North to South trajectories

European literacy in general, not necessarily just initial vernacular literacy, derived mostly from lands initially dominated by Latin and Greek sources. Their vernacular literacies developed over centuries and although many of their corresponding speakers attempted to continue speaking the vernaculars that they read, their written and read realizations often had only meager currency and often regressed into semiclassicals, remaining relatively unchanged even after their vernaculars continued to change and even to be replaced.

Latin had the greatest impact on premodern literacy throughout Europe. It was avowedly spread by 'imperial might, imperial roads and imperial peace'. 'Who would not want to be a Roman?', Cicero asked rhetorically (thereby revealing a view of the changeability of ethnicity which was not widely shared outside of the Roman-impacted world, certainly not until very recent time) and, indeed, the greater Roman codevelopment, modernization and prosperity sphere contributed mightily to the voluntary and involuntary spread of Latin, both in speech and, to a much more limited extent (since literacy itself was initially primarily such a limited phenomenon), in reading/writing.

Since Roman legions took up positions throughout Western Europe over a period of many centuries, the Latinate speech of the Roman legions was necessarily different century after century and province after province *ab initio*. Since the pre-Roman and co-Roman local vernaculars were also obviously different throughout this huge expanse, the local languages that developed throughout the Empire as a result of the interpenetration between these two great but changeable realities, that of the occupiers and that of the occupied, laid the groundwork for widely different resulting urban-based literacies in a variety of related and unrelated languages.

Subsequently, missionaries and commerce also contributed mightily to and solidified the literacies that the Romans had introduced into most of Europe. Simultaneously as well as subsequently, missionaries, commerce and warfare also contributed mightily to, solidified and altered the literacies that the Romans, and those who had Romanness 'bestowed' or forced upon them, had been so instrumental in initiating.

The West to East and the North to South trajectories of the spread of and resistance to literacy in Europe

Much of European literacy (both classical and vernacular) spread during and after the Roman period from larger to smaller urban centers and from smaller urban centers into the countryside. It simultaneously spread from West to East, along with the growth and spread of other societally based innovative processes such as the growth and spread of means of trade, the growth and spread of technology and the growth and spread of modernization more generally. As a result, literacy came to be governed, at least somewhat and at some times, by spatial or geographic co-occurrences. Literacy per se around the world developed first in geospatially more fortunate and socioculturally more stabilized but yet stimulating settings and spread from these to others along the most

The Rise of Vernaculars of Literacy in Europe 33

facilitative trade routes and communication channels. Impassable mountain ranges, large and turbulent bodies of water, daunting deserts and endemic diseases have sometimes been important considerations in connection with the relative absence of such spread around the world, just as have extremes of climate and the resulting voluntary and involuntary movements of native populations, immigration and emigration, economic change and severe dislocations in their sources of livelihood. All of the foregoing have often been major modulators of the spread of vernacular literacy in Europe as well.

If we establish a 2 × 2 table such that the horizontal dimension is dichotomized into West and East along the Germanic vs. Slavic divide, and into North and South at approximately the latitudes of the Alps and the Pyrenees, we then obtain four quadrants (see Figure 3.1) that are extremely

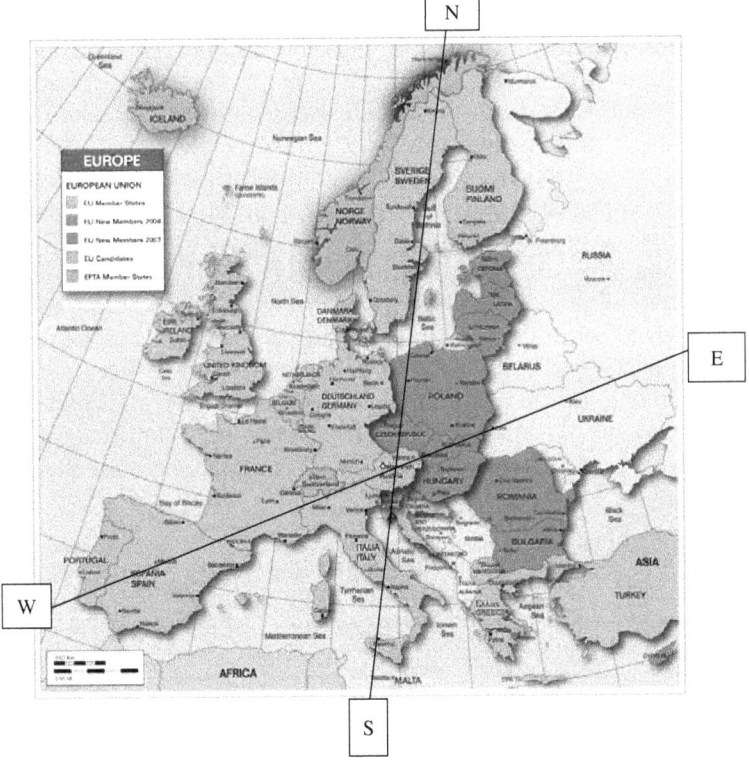

Figure 3.1 Map of Europe showing present boundaries and approximate West–East and North–South Quadrants http://www.nationsonline.org/oneworld/europe_map.html

important spatial parameters in connection with following the rise and development of European vernacular literacies.

A rough four-fold 2 × 2 table may then be superposed on the map that will provide a parsimonious approach to examining the dates at which vernacular literacies were first introduced in various parts of Europe. Even Deutsch's Table 3.1 to which we have referred earlier, with all its admitted imperfections, can be used in this fashion.

Although there are a few noteworthy exceptions, it is generally the case (and demonstrably so from Deutsch's Table 3.1, above) that European vernacular literacy, dating from medieval through to modern times (T2–T4), has spread throughout that continent from West to East and from North to South. Once again, we base this assertion on the data revealed by Deutsch's Table 3.1 which, although it has its imperfections and shortcomings, is one of the very few that provides an overview of the complex matter that is of such central interest to this chapter. Table 3.2 below is derived from the data of Table 3.1 by computing the average time/quadrant in which mass vernacular literacy was introduced across all the languages in that quadrant. It should be pointed out, however, that Table 3.2 is not quite as accurate as it appears to be. The T-periods on which it is based are not equal in length, yet the arithmetic treatment makes them appear to be so. Nor are the quadrants equal in size or in population.

Note that a table such as the above treats each political entry as a unit equal to every other. Both of these contrary-to-fact assumptions are necessary in order to count political units/quadrant, so as to compute average T-times for each quadrant and so as to compute average T-times for each row, column and for the table *in toto*. Nevertheless, even after taking all of these reservations into consideration, the table clearly confirms our initial

Table 3.2 What was the average year (in terms of T-periods) in which mass vernacular literacy was introduced in the four quadrants of the European Continent?

	West	East	Average
North	2.4	3.0	north 2.7
South	2.75	3.9	south 3.325
Average	West: 2.515	East: 3.45	a-T-t 2.99

T-t = Total of totals.

hypotheses (which is to say that the admitted imperfections in the table cannot conceivably be considered the cause for their doing so). Vernacular literacy did arrive in the East of Europe later than in the West; later in the South than in the North. Moreover, the difference between the West and East is greater overall than that between the North and the South. The relatively most advanced quadrant is in the North-West and the most delayed one is in the South-East. There is clearly a spatial/geographic dimension to the arrival of popular vernacular literacy in Europe (and probably elsewhere as well).

But wait a minute! No one can really claim that there is something about 'easterliness' or 'southerliness', per se, that effects the time of acquisition of vernacular literacy. If these innocent spatial dimensions appear to be related to differentials in the onset of European vernacular literacy it must be because they co-occur with certain large-scale societal process variables and, therefore, the former (the spatial dimensions) can be used as first approximations or 'short hand' indications of the latter (the time of arrival of vernacular literacy). The societal process variables may or may not be more in number than the two considerations that we have reviewed in this chapter, but they are certainly more difficult to nail down (to define, to discuss, to document and to analyze) than are the four points of the compass, which is the reason the geographic discussion has preceded the societal dimensions discussion. It is to the latter more difficult task that we will now turn in the next chapter. Thus, this chapter may be regarded as having been a kind of introduction to the examination of societal processes and the next two chapters are intended to take us closer to that goal, at least along a number of dimensions, indices and directions.

Note

1. Although, strictly speaking, some of them also deal with years prior to T2, the following works may all provide additional perspective on the T2 period: Bauman and Greg (1994), Chartier (1989) and Houston (1988).

References

Bauman, A.K. and Greg, W. (1994) *Literacy and Power in the Ancient World*. Cambridge: Cambridge University Press.

Chartier, R. (ed.) (1989) *The Culture of Print: Power and the Uses of Print in Early Modern Europe*. Princeton: Princeton University Press.

Deutsch, K. 1953 (revised 1966) *Nationalism and Social Communication*. Cambridge: MIT Press.

Houston, R.A. (1988) *Literacy in Early Modern Europe: Culture and Education 1500–1800*. London: Longman.
Kloss, H. and McConnell, G.D. (eds) (1974) *Linguistic Composition of the Nations of the World*. Quebec City: Laval University Press.
Price, G. (ed.) (2000) *Encyclopedia of the Languages of Europe*. Oxford: Blackwell.

Chapter 4
Macro-factors in the Societal Spread of Vernacular Literacy

Religions of Literacy

The expression 'vernaculars of literacy' is intended to be a contrastive expression to 'classicals of literacy'. Whereas the latter characterization denotes primarily religious varieties that are no longer spoken (NB: continuity of varietal names does not imply continuity of original varietal functions[1]), the former characterization pertains both to modern vernaculars and their somewhat older precursors which do not quite reach back to the times when their ethnoculture's venerated classical texts were created or 'received'. The very fact that there are many fewer 'classicals of literacy' than 'vernaculars of literacy' (in Europe as well as elsewhere too) implies that there may be many European 'vernaculars of literacy' that lack any direct or indirect link to a 'classical' of their very own. This is, indeed, the case, and particularly in the Germanic field, in which old Anglo-Saxon was geographically too isolated, too ephemeral and too peripheral to wield much influence elsewhere on the continent. Its 'holy functions' never became as central to a 'Great Tradition' as did the texts of the other classical vernaculars of the continent. English lacks any historical and literary link to an ancient, powerful and unifying civilization that spread far and wide beyond its own insular borders. Its current ubiquity and power truly elicits glimpses of miraculous intercession but not of miraculous ancestry.

The fact that the Germanic language family became more distanced from Anglo-Saxon than did any of the Romanic vernaculars of literacy from Latin or any of the Slavic vernaculars of literacy from Old Church Slavonic, may be viewed as related to another development too, namely, that the Germanic lands long lacked a united political center. They experienced the Reformation earlier and more ferociously that did the Romanic or the Slavic lands. The Germanic lands were the original homelands of Protestantism and the Germanic insurrection against Rome came earlier and substantively in more diverse ways than it did elsewhere. The sociocultural conservativism that is the general hallmark of religions also leads to the greater longevity and cross-boundary functionality of their classicals of literacy. Wherever classicals and vernaculars are derived from the same linguistic 'family' and function in the same ethnoculture, it is inevitably the latter that has more recently been adopted for literacy purposes, usually against the opposition of the established Church. Indeed, in some cases the 'classicals of literacy' have substantially delayed ('thwarted'?) the development of corresponding 'vernaculars of literacy' into the 21st century (the case of Arabic being the primary, but far from being the only, example in Europe). The liberation of vernaculars from the literacy monopolies previously exercised by religious classicals alone is certainly an important contextual factor leading to the birth of vernacular literacies in general and to their earlier birth in Europe than on other continents. This 'liberation' is also part and parcel both of social change and of social conflict, a price that Europe has had to pay for its ugly duckling 'precociousness' in conjunction with the worldwide development of vernacular literacies out of their classical cocoons, both through and despite their religious origins.

Today, European literacy is less recognizably a distinctly religious by-product, and particularly so in the Germanic sphere, than the full historical picture 'on the ground' would truly reveal if looked at carefully. None of Europe's very vibrant classical vernaculars of religion are deeply and directly tied to indigenous classicals of the Anglo-Germanic region, but, on the other hand, this region fully confirms the fact that churches can not only be conservers and defenders of old classical and classic-based traditions but also be the defenders and ennoblers of new vernacular literacies and of the ideologies and theologies that are initially dependent upon and long remain preoccupied with them. The famous Anglican 'Book of Common Prayer' (1551) proclaims God's special attachment to English because it is a 'language understood of the people', an article of faith that perfectly fits into the general Germanic-Protestant pro-vernacular tradition and converted that tradition into one of Europe's greatest and most steadfast sources of vernacular (i.e. post-classical) literacies. As Protestantism spread throughout northern and central Europe it quickly established the local state-building (i.e. the central governmental) language of literacy initially derived from its own Great Tradition. Usually kings became the heads of the national state churches. The variety of the newly established vernacular of literacy remained 'religiously' relatively frozen but what was initially the same vernacular remained open to change in other ('secular') everyday functions over the centuries. The English of the 'King James' Version' of the Bible and of the earliest service in the Anglican Church remains the preferred 'religious version' of English in many American Protestant churches to this very day (Ferguson, 1976). In a sense, it has become the 'New Classical' of religious literacy in much of American religious reading, sermonizing and discourse (even in some of American Catholicism), notwithstanding the availability of other Church-approved translations/versions. All in all, therefore, Luther's famous High German translation of the Bible set the stage for all other countries in which Protestantism succeeded in rejecting Latin and in rendering all other vernaculars of 'religion-related reading, sermonizing and singing' into the official vernacular, thereby both effectively killing off the local Latin services as well as establishing both new semiclassicals of religion and new vernaculars of literacy throughout the Protestant world. The original semiclassicals of religion then underwent their own textual sacralizations, leaving the modernizing state vernaculars to attain standardization (and restandardization) on authoritative bases of their own. Sacralization worked both ways in the Protestant world (and not only within Protestanism), on the one hand, it served to undercut the classical language of Shared Western Christendom, and, on the other, to greatly multiply the number of vernaculars of secular literacy (many of which went on over the centuries to maintain and develop both the functions and the structures of new varieties of a semiclassical nature within the religious realm (Fishman, 2007)).

This is not a case of 'history repeating itself'; it is a case of functional differentiation and specificity as a basic sociolinguistic process, even within the relatively unchanging ('eternal') realm of the sacred. Similar processes occur within other religions, and, indeed, in connection within the varieties associated with other societal functions and institutions, religion being the most prominent and powerful among them. Western religions are print-text bound and consensually so. They need a written text and service in the language of the people and of the state. When that language is not yet felt to be excessively archaic and stigmatized as such, the Western churches are among its staunch defenders in most (if not all) sacred functions; when it does come to be regarded as excessively archaic, these churches are likely to beat the path to the door among its rejectionists.

Widespread Sociocultural Change in Nonreligious Pursuits

The birth of vernacular literacies on the Romance languages front

There is a clearer continuity between the classical literacies and the Romance vernacular literacies, than between the former and the Germanic vernacular literacies, if only because the Romance vernacular literacies did have a genuine classical literacy that preceded them and out of which they grew. Indeed, the main problem faced by early Romance literacy efforts was how to go beyond classic literacy and how to attain postclassical (i.e. vernacular) literacies themselves, maintaining, nevertheless their justifiably proud inheritances of classical intimations and derivations. While their non-Romance neighbors often longed for classical origins of their own, many distinguished Romance inheritors on the other hand, often sighed to free themselves of a too burdensome and too transparent classical literacy of their very own. Literacy and literacy efforts differed greatly in the actual and perceived distances of their very own vernaculars from their one and the same classical. Indeed, they viewed their similar if not identical classicals to be equivalent to one another. At roughly one and the same time, some of the advocates of French, Spanish, Portuguese, Occitan, Provençal or Castilian (and, much more subsequently, even Roumanian) considered themselves to be the 'new Latin', the 'reborn Latin' or the 'genuine Latin' of their time and place, others, nevertheless, advocated accepting literacies in their own vernaculars and with their own names. As time passed, both approaches fused and accepted their own unique antiquity as well as understandability, for the same as well as for different functions. Indeed, antiquity and modernity were the two faces of transitional 'Latins for special purposes'.

Religion is merely an example of how social change under its own hierarchic control, slow and halting though it may at times appear to be, constitutes social change nonetheless. More importantly, however, religious change is not an independent factor vis-à-vis language. There are manifold other social forces, particularly in Western societies, that both correspond to, reflect and control religious change. We started our discussion with 'religion' because it is so frequently overlooked as a factor in Europe's, and in the West's manifold experiences of the varietal birth of vernaculars of literacy. The causal nexus between the two is bidirectional and mutual: sometimes some aspects of social change precede language change whereas sometimes it responds to it. In fact, often the two are hard to disentangle. Their nature and their functions are syncretistic. It was not language per se which initially 'changed the societal view of women' in the context of literacy, thereby forcing various segments of society to express this change via how they used language. On the other hand, it is not enough to depend on prior language change if one is an activist who is eager to see sexual biases counteracted in society's treatment of one half of humankind. Planned language change may be necessary but it is still not sufficient in order to independently accomplish desired social change.

Language variety usage *does* reveal the societal views, preferences and biases of speakers, but it is not, by itself, the prior cause of these biases. Certain topics are governed by language taboos, which render us cautious about revealing them. Others are treated so indirectly, so 'societally self-censoredly', as to lead us to our own, individual problem solution rather than to wait for any particular societal problem solution to come to the fore. Language is also used to dissimulate, to hide and to disguise one's true motives and one's basic wishes (particularly in certain social circles, settings and reward constellations), so that it is not linguistic determinism that we are interested in but merely relative linguistic relativism. On the whole, advocates and opponents may speak differently about the same events, particularly in the long run, and most particularly so when they feel free to 'be themselves', in private, when relatively unburdened by self-censorship and when assured of lack of repercussions from their interlocutors. The impact of language (which language?, which variety?, for which point of view?) is highly contextually conditioned and should always be interpreted keeping that in mind. This is a difficult thing to do and is itself strongly conditioned by context. Nevertheless, modern researchers have perfected various measures and corrections for detecting social desirability responses (see Fishman & Galguerra, 2002) and these corrections commonly go at least half-way toward detecting and counteracting such responses. Language use varies contextually and this contextual variation is often pegged to the functional self-interest of speakers and institutions, so that the latter can more effectively exercise their awareness of when and in what direction such self-interest lies. Vernacular literacies, because of their wider availability, have played a major role in that connection.

Changes in leadership, territory, identity and ideology

We usually don't stop to think that human life and its cultural implementation exact a spatial price. Languages too 'require their own space' and any severe changes in the territorial landscapes of human cultures will force changes to occur in their linguistic counterparts as well. Impassable terrain in one direction may force invaders, migrants and explorers to move in another. Later, language or dialect boundaries may or may not remain as fixed as territorial borders once were (before bridges, superhighways, trains, automobile transportation, sea-going vessels and air routes became widely available). The Germanic–Romanic spoken languages border has remained relatively fixed along the Rhine for over a thousand years, even though the political borders (and the governmental and school languages that pertain to them) have changed many times in reaction to the outcome of wars and treaties. Alsatian (a language variety of Alsace), Letzembourgisch (a language variety of Luxembourg) and Flemish (a language variety of Belgium and the Netherlands) would probably have different functions today – including different literacy-related functions – had their histories been different, even if their populations had remained ethnically very much as they are today. Varieties of literacy are by-products of *force majeure* 'on the ground' and varieties that are or could have been, have lived and died by the sword, but not just by the sword alone. The birth and death of languages are not DNA-governed and expanding or aggressive languages at time T1 do not necessarily remain so at time T2 or T3. Ideologies develop out of time-bound experiences and their interpretations of these experiences may be lingua-centric or lingua-peripheral. No one can dispute the fact that lingua-centric ideologies are fostered by grievances between neighboring and linguistically different cultures, but the hostilities that develop out of such grievances need not be mutually hostile or similarly lingua-centric. The Franco-German tale of endless grievances, bloodshed, rivalry and competition which have kept Europe full of plots, counterplots and insults throughout pretty much the quarter century when the Franco-Prussian War occurred, circumstances which both Great Britain and Czarist Russia exploited over and over again to tilt the balance of power in the direction of their own best interests, are cases in point.

Nevertheless, both England and Russia recognized far greater virtues with respect to the French (on the part of England) and toward Germany (on the part of Russia) than did the two continental superstars with respect to one another. Paris was the 'other capital of European culture' for the British, just as Berlin was the capital of European science and technology for the Moscovites to watch, emulate and imitate. And all of the foregoing transpired even though the second millennium started off with the Treaty of Strassburg in which each of Charlemagne's elder sons promised to keep the peace, recognized each other's major language and granted one another the right to address the other in the other's mother tongue and to do so in public at that. Thus did the Rhine guarantee military peace between the two great powers who bordered it, but also guaranteed that their cultural and linguistic animosity would be safe to continue forever. None of the little languages along the Rhine (in Luxembourg, Flanders, Alsace, Lorraine and German Switzerland) was ever permitted to independently disturb the peace, that privilege being exclusively preserved for French and German. Political and ideological pacts can restrict or stabilize the development of 'languages of literacy', on the one hand, as well as to constantly lead to their explosive eruption and displacement on the other.

Nevertheless, strange as it may seem, there are also successful transborder arrangements, for example, the distinctly political (rather than cultural) border between the Netherlands and Belgium, proclaiming both of their Germanic varieties to be different renditions of the same literacy-related Netherlandic tongue (so that all decisions as to the latter's spelling, grammar, vocabulary, etc.) that can be settled amicably by a bi-governmental committee on which each side of the border is equally represented. Also, Valencian and Catalan have recently set aside their century-long dispute as to whether they are really two different languages, or merely two different dialects of the same language (Catalan). It would appear that in Europe, at least, political and ideological points of view have occasionally been invoked in order to restrict the proliferation of territorially officialized varieties, rather than to increase them. But all of Europe has not proceeded in this manner. Poland has been slowly chipped away by its neighbors (Austro-Hungary, Russia and newly nascent Imperial Germany), until, at last, it was gone entirely and the future of its major language appeared to many 'loyal sons' to be under threat. The Scandinavian lands came under one or another's control at different times during the 17th through 19th centuries, The Balkans became synonymous with interminable and insoluble interlinguistic and intralinguistic contention, as languages, religions and states alternatively coincided and parted company (and might still do so today if they were left to their own devices), becoming known as the 'tinder-box of Europe' because of its inflammatory role in inciting not only hostilities but in leaving behind unprecedented ethnoreligious borders as well as previously unknown ethnolinguistic ones. Europe was still full of lost mother tongues and regained fatherlands throughout the 19th century – each one of which defined newly privileged and unprivileged language commitments and revengeful goals and obligations. Having the 'right language' and speaking, reading and writing it in the right way (alphabet, spelling, grammar, punctuation) became major desiderata for millions of Europeans who were considered to be not only poor foreigners (as they might well have been in some other century), but, as enemies and deracinated destroyers and deniers of their own erstwhile kin and potential sources of comfort, aid and support, all the foregoing influenced degrees and type faces of literacies.

Warfare, holocaust and other unusually destructive acts of man or God

The placement of the present topical concern for 'purposeful destruction', coming as it does after the one prior to it, is not meant to signal a step upward on some scale of horror, injury, or particular negativity of impact. The Roman destruction of its neighbor and rival in trans-Mediterranean commerce was the great, feared and, indeed, ferocious city-state-empire on the north-central coast of Africa: Carthage. Since familiarity does not necessarily breed respect (it merely provides opportunities for respect to develop, 'among the other things' that the passage of time may facilitate), the tenor of the interactions between these two great powers slowly but surely descended from bad to worse. They had to learn to share control of what both considered to be 'Mare Nostrum' – the shared Mediterranean Sea – but what could have become a pioneering adventure in cross-cultural creativity ultimately became a tale of agony that has not subsided during the two millennia that separates 'then' from 'now' (for both circum-Mediterranean Europeans and circum-Mediterranean Africans).

This tale ends not merely with the sacking and burning of Carthage, including its literally incomparable and irreplaceable library of ancient (Berber) writings – a form of retribution so obviously fated that both Rome and Alexandria experienced it too in due time – but with the additional obliteration of anything and everything that remained to mark its former site. Only a vast and barren desert remained to bear witness that a distinct and distinctive literacy had been struck dumb, a literacy that would regain its life and voice among the languages of its region only in our own generation, when Berber reading and writing (and publishing!) were reborn (Ennaji, 1997) to grapple with the uncertainties of latecomers. We must not permit our fascination with other and more pleasant scenarios (around which courses, texts and conferences can be stylishly designed), to lead us to overlook this, for from the days of Ozimandias to our own Soviet, Balkan and Chinese 'resettlement and natural reconstruction' projects, not to mention the infamously almost successful 'final solution' project of the Germans and their collaborators, it is precisely such scenarios of utter and wanton destruction that predominate in the annals of language life and death. The Americas are by no means exempt from this sad observation, nor is there any reason to conclude that the well of tears will run dry on any continent in the near future. Speakers of the little indigenous languages south of the Rio Grande, or those along the Euphrates corridor, many of whom possessed ancient and hallowed literacy traditions now lost and generally forgotten, are hardly likely to interpret our destructive presence in their midst, as a boon to their future developmental recovery.

The West to East Trajectory in the Rise of Vernacular Languages of Literacy

Americans have very odd assumptions regarding Europe. Spreading out a large map of Europe, they normally view it from East to West, just as they do with a map of the United States, as if that were the normal direction of development on all continents and at all times. But the directionality of development is not fixed by some mysterious magnetic pole. It is what it is, because of circumstances and influences that may be quite local and idiosyncratic and therefore different in Siberia than in Friesland. In connection with our concern for the birth and death of languages of literacy, there is actually considerable West to East growth to account for. Setting aside the classicals, for the moment, and turning to Table 3.2 (which, if the reader remembers, is read from West to East) we may ask why this particular progression should have occurred (quite an orderly one indeed for a huge continent-wide development)? We might speculate that a lingering role of the Roman Empire was involved (by far the greater part of the Empire lay West of the Rhine), or that Catholicism was somehow involved (by far the greater part of the European Catholic heartland is found in this area), but the hypothesis that makes fewest assumptions about holy intercessions is simply that 'secular literacy follows trade'. The great modern ports of Europe were initially Western European and it is from them that the colonial conquests in Africa and in the New World, colonial trade, the commercial revolution and the industrial revolution all initially sprang. The lubricant that speeds the wheels on which gods, goods, gold and human bondage travel, are not so much the Vulgate of the priest as the account books of the entrepreneurs, the bills of lading, the bills payable and receivable, and the 'bets' as to future prices and the fluctuations relative to current ones. Atlantic ports had long been prominent in intra-European growth, but with the discovery of the New World and better means of both sea and land transportation the new routes to the Indies that they had long traveled now received a new lease of life, far beyond the Middle East, which still attracted them vigorously. No wonder that capitals and ports and the languages that served them and 'made them work' became the earliest carriers, defenders and protagonists of European national literacies.

The obvious next step in the expansion of European hegemony over intercontinental trade lay in the shipping prowess of the former Hanseatic

League (the Netherlands and Northern Germany), the Danish, Swedish, Finnish, Baltic 'box', the Danubian access to the foregoing in the North, as well as to the Black Sea in the South, and the long semidormant ports of Italy and the Adriatic. Their contact with the New World was much weaker than that of the Western and North-Western ports, but their ties with North Africa, the Near East, Central Asia and South and South-East Asia were vastly extended by the burgeoning technological growth of the 16th century. On the continent itself, the Germanic world (essentially from Scandinavia to the Alps) experienced a flowering of city life, city production and city culture that was every bit as advanced as that attained *and maintained* by the West of Europe a century earlier. That century's hiatus ultimately made a great difference, not so much in the rise and fall of languages of literacy (that too) but in the consolidation of rivalries and competition with respect to overseas colonies, trade routes, trade partners and world influence that all of the foregoing yielded. While the West plundered the riches of Africa, Asia and the Americas, Germany and Italy scrambled to even get a hold of bits and pieces of the foregoing that they could call their own (until subsequent wars robbed them even of such control as they had). These deeply imbedded rivalries and hostilities also helped English abroad to become the language of modernization (with its notoriously gloved hand vis-à-vis colonial literacies), in competition with Germany, just as it later helped German consolidate and expand its advantages vis-à-vis even later suitors in Africa, while indirectly fostering the advancement of Afrikaans (in South Africa), Swahili (in Tanzania) and even Flemish (in the 'Belgian Congo'). Thus did the rise of literacy in the home countries help determine the rise of European vernaculars of literacy in colonial contexts outside of Europe and their subsequent roles on the world scene.

The Role of the Spread of Religion, Philosophy and Style of Life in the Rise of New Languages

The impact of the spread of Religion, which we have already looked at, is not that different from the spread of new technologies more generally, insofar as the birth or death of languages is concerned. It is important, indeed, to realize that both material and subjective factors may move populations to abandon prior beliefs and practices (and the languages through which they are expressed or enacted) in very similar ways. The major difference between these two sets of causal determinants is that religion can more frequently 'cut both ways', that is, move events toward the rise of a new language (even a totally new language, rather than just one that is territorially and demographically new in certain contexts while it remains fully 'at home' and fully indigenized elsewhere) as well as moving them toward the demise of an old one. Thus, the rise of Yiddish among Ashkenazim (Jews in or [ancestrally] from Central Europe) in 11th century Alsace-Lorraine, for the purposes of textual translation and commentary among male students, obviously occurred without any immediate impact on the La'az or Chuadit that women members of the Worms, Mainz and Schpier communities were already speaking at the time and that they had brought with them from France or Northern Italy (M. Weinreich, 1980 [1973]). However, the continued use of Yiddish led not only to its subsequent displacement of the prior Jewish vernaculars among males, subsequent to their bilingualization, but also to their displacement among females as well in that function (everyday speech), even though the latter long lacked a language of literacy of their own.

The spread of languages into 'new' areas and populations due to the spread of religions is well known and has had a long and rich history behind it. To begin with, only Latin and Old Church Slavonic were of European provenience, whereas both Hebrew and Arabic were 'imported' into Europe from the Middle East and/or from North Africa. However, in both respects, that is, whether internally generated or externally forced, the languages of large-scale material change 'behave' exactly as disruptively as do the languages that accompany religious spread and religious change. The introduction of the horse into the Americas, the introduction of Christianity, the introduction of the motor, the introduction of capitalism, the introduction of electricity and the introduction of atomic power (for civilian use) have all had similarly dislocative, disruptive and destructive impacts on some languages and have provided greater and more powerful opportunities and advantages for others. The story of the birth and death of languages is part and parcel of the story of social change more generally. It is no more possible to keep vernacular language from changing, constantly and everywhere, than it is to keep sociocultural change from taking place. The rise and fall of languages is merely one aspect of an apparently endless story of an eternally restless species that itself causes most of the changes that engulf it.

There is no calling a halt to the changes in the status quo ante, even by movements that seek to outlaw or restrict social change. Spoken Pennsylvania German (often referred to today as 'Pennsylfanisch') has changed remarkably during its 300+ years of relative isolation from 'the world' since its arrival in the United States. Indeed, at times the reluctance to change becomes identified with a speech variety of a community's own, whether in speech or in script, namely the 'Hindustani' (the usual name for Hindi during Gandhi's lifetime) of

Mahatma Gandhi's movement to return to traditional cottage industries. This identification of a major 'return to nature' movement with a new designation of an unviolated language variety led inevitably to the choice of a different name ('Hindi') for the variety of the India Union Party and its far-flung efforts to liberate, unify, modernize, de-caste and democratize India and even the Indian diaspora. The very acts of sociocultural liberation lead to new linguistic dissolution for some and to linguistic supremacy convictions for others. There is no language policy which is beneficial for everyone on both sides of whatever econopolitical divide that may exist and contextualize (render meaningful) the changes that have taken place or are instituted.

The Dampening Effect of a Much Stronger and Already Widely Known Neighbor That Is Very Similar to Its Weaker Cognate

Linguists generally look to language factors per se in their efforts to explain the status change of languages. The foregoing catalog of megafactors represents an effort to disabuse students of any tendency along such lines. Languages are not merely proprioceptive. They do not respond only to the stimuli or characteristics that they themselves emit. Nevertheless, they are not merely causally inert bodies either, that is, bodies that merely react to characteristics of their speakers or to those of their speakers' neighbors. In the rise and fall of languages, there are sometimes characteristics of the languages themselves which must be considered co-causal in the fate that befalls them.

One such co-causal influence on the future of a language, for example, in whether or not a given variety is ever considered 'literacy appropriate' is whether it is sufficiently autonomous to carry both the burdens and the honors of literacy. If its candidacy for literacy has arisen later than that of its neighbors, these neighbors per se may be considered 'more worthy' in the eyes of God or in the eyes of learned users for such higher status. Such 'lateness to literacy', however, is not merely a self-caused or self-initiated dimension. It too must also have its own external causes, such as the more fortunate neighbor's greater proximity to centers of commerce, greater access to natural resources that can be utilized to support schools, teachers and learners, greater exposure to still other varieties that are accompanied by writing systems that have already gained quite a regional following (as e.g. have Latin script, Cyrillic script, Arabic script, Devanagari script, etc., in connection with print-related hardware) and so on.

More important than any of the foregoing – and more environmentally responsive as well – is the degree of structural similarity between the two varieties, the stronger predecessor and the weaker latecomer to literacy. When this similarity obtains it is common for the latter to be viewed as merely a dialect of the former (see Chapter 2, above) and the loss of print and literacy functions of their own is one of the first sacrifices that dialects must frequently make. 'Dialects are for conversations between family and friends, not for governmental, legal, scientific and religious formalities'. The latter is such a widespread view that one of the first things that literacy champions undertake to accomplish along the path of their literacy advocacy for Variety X is to increase the numbers and the magnitudes of its 'differences' (grammatical, orthographic, lexical and scriptal) from the usages that typify Variety Y. Valencian was until very recently purposely 'built away' from Catalan, as was (and also until recently) Flemish from Dutch. Still ongoing are the efforts to increase the authenticity ('uniqueness') of Frisian vis-à-vis Netherlandish, Yiddish vis-à-vis German, Russyn vis-à-vis Ukrainian, Croatian vis-à-vis Serbian and so on. These are all 'ausbau' languages (languages which have been modified by human intervention) whose supporters are convinced that increased visual and auditory difference between themselves and the 'enemy' will foster their chances of being accepted for H functions, as literacy-worthy in all respects. Sometimes political factors intervene (as in the case of Valencian and Flemish) and solve the struggle, for the time being, in favor of one side or the other (the losers accepting a dialect status in spoken functions). Croatian is now official in the newly founded Croatia and may be expected to foster Ausbau to its heart's content in the immediate future (as will Montenegran and Bosnian). Yiddish and Russyn have still not received the politico-linguistic support that would fully satisfy the self-concepts of their true believers. There are still varieties in Europe that have no official functions in the EU. In recent years, Catalan, Basque, Gallego and Asturian (all in Spain), and Irish (but not yet Scotts-'Gollik') have all been given a smidgeon of recognition, but there are still some two dozen varieties that have had no satisfaction whatsoever and the vast majority are Ausbaudependent if they are to attain literacy.

Were Afrikaans speakers to have been relocated en masse to the Netherlandish-German border over a century, its history would have been more problematic there than it was in the depths of South Africa with 'only' the linguistically more different English to compete with (at the same time many Blacks viewed it as a doorway to White opportunities). In comparison, Letzembourgish has long attained separate official recognition within Luxembourg (which also recognizes German and French), although Letzembourgish has never been nominated for the EU status that Catalan and Asturian have just attained in Spain, without attaining any kind of nationwide role such as Letzembourgish has in Luxembourg.

Both of these scenarios emphasize the nonlinearity (non-'scalability') of the position of the weaker variety within an Ausbau relationship. Several dozen such varieties have already been lost between varieties that have competed with each other in Europe during the past few centuries. Functional competition is difficult enough for the weak, but to have to also compete structurally as well at the same time, is quite a burden to bear. As King Solomon once said, 'It is far better to be young, rich and strong than otherwise', or at least to be thought so, or at the very least, to think so of oneself. Good advice, but seldom attainable.

Note

1. New names have been suggested for modern vernacular Greek and vernacular Hebrew: Demotic and Israeli. If these names become more widely accepted, both at home and abroad, they may ultimately pose the problem of whether new languages have been born there or old ones have been renamed when used for more modern functions.

References

Anon. (1983) *The Fairest Flower: The Emergence of National Consciousness in Renaissance Europe*. Firenzem L'Acaemia della Crusca.
Deutsch, K.W. (1943) The trend of European Nationalism: The language aspect. *American Political Science Review* (36), 533–541.
Ferguson, C.A. (1976) *The Role of the English of the King James Bible in American Christianity* (p. 148). New York: Oxford University Press.
Kloss, H. and McConnell, G.D. (eds) (1974) *Linguistic Composition of the Nations of the World*. Quebec City: Laval University Press.
Kloss, H. and McConnell, G.D. (eds) (1978) *The Written Languages of the World: A Survey*. Quebec City: Laval University Press.
Price, G. (ed.) (2000) *Encyclopedia of the Languages of Europe*. Oxford: Blackwell.

Chapter 5
Heroes of European Vernacular Literacy

Charles A. Ferguson, the preeminent sociolinguist of the 20th century, long planned to write a volume to be entitled 'Prophets (or, alternatively, 'Saints') of Literacy'. This volume, which he was regrettably unable to bring to anywhere near completion, was to be devoted largely to the Christian clergy who carried literacy to distant parts of the globe and to languages and cultures of which Europe hitherto had almost no knowledge and even little or no awareness. The current volume has gained substantially from my readings of and discussions with Ferguson over many years, and the two volumes, one planned but never realized and one now en route to realization, are therefore related and even similar to some degree. Mine is both more Eurocentric and less focused on Christianity and on linguistics than Ferguson's would most likely have been. Nevertheless this chapter is affectionately dedicated to his memory and to his stimulation.

My 'four heroes of European vernacular literacy' are distributed across several centuries and across Europe, from West to East. None of them was really a linguist, as the term is generally understood today (although one came close to that pursuit via folklore study), and none of them were 'men of the cloth' at the time of their greatest efforts on behalf of vernacular literacy. The four to whom I am referring are, 'from left to right', Nebrija, Gutenberg, Vuk and Lefin. Whosoever does not know their names or their attainments on behalf of vernacular literacy within their own cultural spheres does not really know European history and culture as a whole.

Antonio de Nebrija (1441-1522)

As must be obvious from his dates, the work of Nebrija transpired before the age of print had begun (if we take as the beginning of the latter to be the year in which Johann Gutenberg's first printed work appeared, 1455). Not only were Nebrija's first works written in Latin, but his very name derives from a self-initiated Latinization of his birth name (Antonio Martínez de Calá). Nevertheless, like his famous Italian predecessor Dante Alighierre (1265–1321), Nebrija became a protagonist on behalf of the language of the common people of Spain (which he referred to as 'vulgara' and 'eloquente', just as Dante had risen to the defense of the 'eloquencia vulgari' in his own setting).

Although best remembered as a linguist (focusing on Spanish grammar and on orthography), he was also a teacher of Latin and, above all, a 'Humanist', that is, a devotee of poetry and rhetoric, the liberal arts, sciences and philosophy, as they were known together in his day and age to a large number of European 'gentlemen and savants'. His defenses of Spanish at a time when Latin reigned supreme (and when Spanish itself was known in the best circles as 'the new Latin') are now shrouded or embroidered by legendry (e.g. upon presenting his *Gramatica Castellans* (1492, in the very year that the New World was discovered) to Queen Isabel I of Castille ('la Católica'), to whom it was dedicated, she is said to have asked him 'Why would I want such a work as this one, since I already know the language?', he is said to have answered 'Your highness, language is the instrument of empire!'), but it is clear that they also not infrequently embroiled him in acrimonious debate with Church authorities in various venues, based as they were on his independent interpretations flowing in no small part from linguistic analyses. Nevertheless, he outlasted his opponents and began to earn a reputation for loyalty to Castile (although he himself was from Andalucia, in the south of Spain). He is said to have advised Columbus to 'subdue the new lands not by force of arms but by naming them', although he was by no means totally above the ethnic nationalism of Spain in his time. Although he believed that internally Spanish was still very far from being rule-governed, still exposed to many changes that might attempt to influence it, and, therefore, still in a semisavage state, its external situation fortunately appears to be quite favorable, because language has always been the companion of empire and with empire, peace always arrives, creating the fine arts and good taste. So it was in Ancient Greece and in Rome and, therefore, Nebrija reasons, 'it can be predicted that with the empire of Isabella and Ferdinand there will come a period of cultural splendor. The Catholic Royalty has united the limbs and the pieces of Spain, has cleansed the faith of impurities (by expelling the Jews and establishing the Inquisition), vanquished the Moors (via completing the Reconquista of the Iberian Peninsula, which had dragged on for centuries), instituted justice, promulgated laws.

Nothing is lacking other than the flourishing of the arts of peace and among the foremost of these, those that teach us the language' (quoting and paraphrasing, Anon. 1983).

Nebrija contributes something crucial to the profile of 'heroes of popular literacy': a political sensitivity derived from a recognition that cultural heroes are inevitably ahead of their times and exposed to forces other than those that they can muster or control, be they sacred or secular. If Nebrija smacks something of sycophancy, that is both because he foresaw the rise of one of the greatest empires that the world had ever known or would yet know, on the one hand, and recognized that only the strong, mighty and wealthy could bring about the popular literacy, good taste and refined culture that were his ultimate goal as fitting companions for the language of a great people that was just coming into being. We are too much creatures of 'post hoc, ergo propter hoc': we too easily forget that neither Spain nor Spanish existed as yet and only a regime that could be counted on to bring them about could really be counted upon to institute and ultimately insist upon widespread popular literacy in the language of the people. Over and over again we note that our heroes of literacy are stymied by the vicissitudes of the ordinary course of current events. After he embarked on his career as a champion of popular literacy he never again had to escape and go into hiding (as he had done several times during his younger years) because of the wrath or animosity of authorities whom he had angered or displeased. Nevertheless, a certain sense of danger is just a little below the surface of Nebrija's life. His oft-mentioned longing for peace as the *summum bonum* of popular literacy proved harder to attain than did popular literacy in the language of the people on whose behalf and for the greater glory of which it was sought. History may have no ultimate purpose, but human beings often do. We would do an injustice to our heroes if we neglected to point this out, as they go through the endless contortions that both public purposes and private purposes force upon us all, be we heroes or not. Nebrija's fearfulness and currying of favor were not assuaged by the amazing and widely acknowledged successes of his history, grammar and phonology. Uneasy lies the head that wears the crown in the kingdom of words. It is simply a fact that needs to be acknowledged.

Johann Gutenberg (1390(?)-1468)

For a very few years the lives of our two first heroes overlapped, but they are actually very different in most respects other than contemporaneity. Nebrija worked mostly with his nimble tongue and pen, while Gutenberg was primarily an inventive mechanic and artistic metal-worker who worked primarily with his hands and imagination. Nebrija was a man of considerable culture and refinement, while Gutenberg was merely of solid middle-class urban mercantile background whose formal learning was meager and did not extend into the secondary level, as distinct from Nebrija's ample background in the classical tongues and in the broad sweep of the Humanities. Perhaps as a result of differences such as these, Gutenberg never successfully engraced himself with the local nobility nor with the Church (although not for want of trying to do so in either case, in attempting to find adequate support for his most promising and expensive inventive efforts). Many of the differences and the similarities between them are importantly attributable to differences between the conditions of their homelands and mother tongues. Spain was perhaps the first major Western state to achieve full geographic unification and linguistic standardization and officialization, while Germany was among the very last. Spain had not yet resigned from any dreams of controlling the European continent, Germany was nothing but a congerie of principalities, duchies, fiefdoms and medieval antiquarian remains that were still centuries away from either political or linguistic self-discovery and lebensraum dreams. Nebrija could therefore dream that his linguistic and literacy goals would be increasingly adopted and exported across the seas, Gutenberg characteristically put his faith not so much in his words as in his machines.

It is one of the ironies of history that Nebrija's great promise of worldwide victories yet to come soon turned to dust and fell onto inhospitable ground. German literacy, on the other hand flourished and soon became a model both to the Western and the Eastern European cultural spheres. Although both had to contend with haughty French cultural dominance, a dominance that often led the two into close cultural ties with one another, Germany became and has remained the very heart of Europe and Spain is still something of a cultural and technological backwater. In our current computer-dominated age (the computer being the great-grandchild and reinvention or reincarnation of the printing press), it is, of course, Gutenberg whose name is known to every high-school student everywhere, whereas Nebrija's is hardly known at all. Thus does technology conquer the humanities in modern times!

The art of printing spread quickly across Europe. By the end of the 15th century (Gutenberg's '12-line Bible' having appeared in 1455) Germany had witnessed some 300 printings, Venice alone had 150 (producing $c.4500$ titles) and according to one estimate, as many as 20 million copies were printed, more than had been produced by all the scribes of Europe in the previous 1500 years. Throughout all of this, Gutenberg himself remains a shadowy figure. The date of his birth is uncertain. None of his printed works bears his name. No portrait of him was done in his lifetime. The little that is known about him has been deduced from a handful of legal documents (e.g. business disputes, loans, annuities, interest defaults, wine-tax payments and a breach of promise suit, and from the 49 remaining copies of his Bible after his death). Indeed, a semifictional account of his life reads more like a novel than like the biography of a man's life. His importance to the rise of popular (vernacular) literacy can only be grasped if we keep in mind that his was the third one of the four turning points in written communication over the past 5000 years (the other three being, first of all, the invention of writing, which permitted the creation of large and enduring societies and priestly or scribal elites; second the invention(s) of the alphabet, which brought writing within the reach of ordinary people; and fourth the coming of the computer and the internet, which represented a further advance in the process of mechanization that had previously yielded the third turning point – the invention of printing from movable type, had burst unto Europe and then the whole world only about 550 years previously, and has been the *sine qua non* of vernacular literacy ever since)[1].

Actually, 'all' that Gutenberg provided on behalf of the third innovation (above) ingredients, was the sparks that fused several previously present ingredients. In many ways, it was an invention that was waiting to happen and it ended the millennia during which scribes had been the main undergirdings for the spread of knowledge and power. The days of the scribes vanished much more quickly than did the days of the secretaries with the coming of the desk computer (some of the latter still being to be found even today). No one has calculated how much more MS-productivity has been fostered by the desk computer but there is a comparative estimate for the printing press. Whereas previously it had taken a month or two to scribally produce a single copy of a book, by the next year 500 copies was the average print-run, for 500 copies could be produced in one week's time. In 1455 all of Europe's printed books could have been carried in a single wagon. Some 50 years later, the titles ran to tens of thousands (28,360 according to one count) and some individual volumes were printed in the millions of copies and the end is not in sight (even though their production via moveable type may very well have begun to decline in the Western world due to the increasing utilization of computer-generated copying methods provided through the internet). Having been the first to produce a printed copy of the Christian Bible, Gutenberg is per force also the father of the Reformation (which blew Christian unity apart forever), and the father of popular vernacular literature worldwide and, as such, the major progenitor of the collapse of classical literature in the Western world. However, Gutenberg is also the major figure in the initial split between the 'two cultures' of which C. P. Snow wrote in the 70s of the previous century. It is a wind that blows both good and bad, as most storms do. For better or for worse, it has replaced 'cogito ergo sum' (Decarte's maxim) by 'scripto ergo sum', a dubious blessing from which the world may never recover. Although initially all of Gutenberg's books were still in Latin, it required but a brief pause before vernacular books began appearing.

Even so, opposition was not slow to develop and some of the very earliest book printers may have been driven out of what was then Europe's largest university for 'consorting with the devil'. The university and the Church were closely allied, of course, and the Church had been on guard against heresy well before the arrival of vernacular literacy. However, the full brunt of the Church's opposition came on the heels of Luther's apostasy, soon after the appearance of Gutenberg's first ('20-line') Bible (still in Latin). The Reformation also originally arose in the German lands, originating not too far from Mainz, where the cradle of the moveable type-press was originally erected. Luther's Bible was in 'sublime' German and though it was not written in a variety identical to any kind of spoken German of that or any other time, it fully deserves the credit for spurring the beginning of widespread vernacular literacy in Europe.

'Vuk' (Vuk Stefanovic Karadzic): (1787-1864)

Among all those who are interested in vernacular literacy the name and fame of our third hero ('Vuk', wolf), for so his fellow-Serbs affectionately called him are far less known than the names and attainments of either of our two Western heroes. This is so, notwithstanding the fact that he functioned some 300 years later than they did, that is much closer to our modern times. There are several reasons for this apparent disparity, the foremost among them being that his 'oyster' was that of the Southern Slavs and that he was neither Catholic nor Protestant, as were Nebrija and Gutenberg respectively, but, rather, Eastern Orthodox more generally and Serbian-Orthodox in particular. It was a part of Europe that was then still dominated by the slowly receding Ottoman Empire and, therefore, far removed in history, culture, religion and ethos from that of the more quickly modernizing West. With all of the regional fame that he attained as the foremost linguist, language reformer and folklorist of the Serbs, he never attained overly much outside recognition except among other South Slav intellectuals (later to be divided into Slovenes, Serbians, Croatians, Montenegrins and Bosnians), on the one hand, and among German intellectuals (both in Germany proper and in the Austro-Hungarian Dual Monarchy), on the other. The link between Vuk and the Germans was a particularly strong one, because of the penetration of the work of the folkloric and linguistic work of the brothers Grim, on the one hand, and of the abiding influence of the social and cultural philosopher Johan Gustav Herder, on the other, throughout the Balkan lands. The Germans considered the South Slavs in particular as their own destined sphere of influence, both culturally and politically, and it was there that foreign and domestic Germanophiles and Russophiles struggled endlessly for supremacy from the 18th to the 20th century, only to be defeated, both of them, by a combination of world events and of local nationalisms.

Linguistic barriers to vernacular literacy in the 18th century Balkans

A parallel to the problem that Latin represented to vernacular literacy in the West of Europe was the problem that Old Church Slavonic represented in most of Eastern Orthodox Europe. The two were not equally obdurate impediments, however, for Western Christendom, as both secular and the spiritual heir of the Western Roman Empire, had attained a unity of form and outlook far beyond any that was known to the Eastern Empire. Although both Latin and Old Church Slavonic were the languages of widespread and supra-ethnic religions, the latter never achieved the degree of standardization (not even for religious purposes) attained by the former. To begin with, Old Church Slavonic was a much younger entity (the split between the Western and the Eastern Catholic Churches not having occurred until the 16th century) and had simply not had as much time to come into being and to assert its sway as had Latin. But the Eastern lands, never having been fully part of the Roman Empire, had themselves retained more of a tolerance of local variation and even self-determination than was the way of the West. Pretty much the same set of geographic, economic, demographic and cultural factors that delayed Eastern urbanization, industrialization and, hence, modernization also delayed the full consolidation of Church Slavonic, but yet it remained a nonvernacular, regionally and chronologically varying and archaic barrier to popular vernacular literature. It was the chief barrier that Vuk had to cope with. Although he did not directly pursue Serbian independence (such advocacy would have damaged chances for either Austrian or Russian support without which much of his already frequently penurious life would have been rendered even more difficult), it is no exaggeration to say that Serbian independence was greatly facilitated by the full local and, ultimately, continent-wide recognition of Serbian linguistic independence, greatness and self-worth that Vuk fostered and unabashedly invited, announced, defended and propogated. Thus in many ways, Vuk was a spearhead of a linguistic, cultural, national and even political revolution which fostered popular literacy in many ways, both directly and indirectly. Indeed, popular literacy has the potential to simultaneously unite and transform the two major ideological systems of modernity: nationalism and globalization.

The Serbian setting

By the beginning of the second millennium (B.C.) the Slavs had already been migrating northward through the Balkans, from the region of Salonika, on the Greek peninsula (where they had dwelled during the days of Cyril and Methodius who had first brought them within the Christian [then Catholic] fold) for many hundreds of years. In part, this massive population movement may have been part of the general westward movement of Asian populations into Europe that had already begun during the days of the Roman Empire. More closely related to our interest in Vuk is the fact that in 1813, when he was but 25 years old, the Moslem Turks recommenced their earlier attempts to occupy and convert the Balkans. As Ottoman troops poured in, and as both Austria and Russia were preoccupied with the final struggle with Napoleon and began to ponder how to stem the Turkish advance and save the Balkans (both for Christianity and, to be sure, for themselves), tens of thousands of Serbians crossed over into the northern Balkan lands of the Austro-Hungarian Empire. As a result, the young Vuk came much more under German linguistic, folkloristic and more generally Viennese intellectual influence than might otherwise have been the case.

In the newly independent Serbia that had arisen in 1804, after defeating the earlier Turkish occupiers, the indigenous leadership was almost totally without book learning and, indeed, had to be convinced that it was a good and even necessary thing. Being of immediate peasant background himself, it became Vuk's mission in life to defend the riches of Serbian authenticity and, at the same time, to synthesize them with Western intellectual thinking and methods of humanistic research. In that very year Vuk first met much better educated north-Balkan 'Slavonic' or 'Illyrian' linguists (the names and identities of many South-Slavic languages and ethnic identities were still somewhat fluid at that time) and they were the conduits through which the Herderian emphases on folk culture (as distinct from literary culture), folk spirit (Volksgeist) and vernacular language (Volkssprache) reached and captured his heart and mind. It was particularly one of them, Jerney Kopitar, whose literary program Vuk dedicated himself to realizing for the remainder of his life some 50 years later. Although he gained thereby the bitter antagonism of the Serbian Orthodox Church (and a few other Serbian leaders), Vuk hewed close to his original goal of fashioning a new Serbian literary norm that was close to the form in which it was spoken (and therefore recognizably different from the somewhat revised and indigenized Serbian Slavonic favored by the Church). This was a decisive choice on Vuk's part and it resulted in rendering much more difficult his struggle to gain acceptance for his subsequently revised Serbian orthography (including simplifications as well as the dropping of a number of old Slavonic letters) which had the further effect of breaking the direct linguistic and cultural links that had until then existed to literary Russian and, which, of course caused the loss of many additionally possible sources of support. His doggedly combative and uncompromising spirit ('peasantlike tenacity and single mindedness' some have called it) is also evident in all else that he undertook: a 'people's primer' of the Serbian language (in which people were admonished to write as they speak), collections of Serbian folktales, folksongs and epic poetry (much praised by Jakob Grimm and by Johann Goethe), a Serbian dictionary, a German–Serbian dictionary and a new Serbian translation of the Evangeium (New Testament). The foundational role of many of the above creations in fostering vernacular literacy among Serbs was obvious and immediately so, even during his own quite short lifetime.

The greater significance and impact of Vuk

The combination of Westernization ('Europeanization') and cultural ethnonationalism is a gift (or a burden) that Eastern Europe has presented to the rest of the continent and even to the rest of the world. The ultimate defeat of one of Vuk's early ('Kopitarian') visions of drawing all the south Slavic languages closer together (particularly Serbian and Croatian) is merely a sign that one cannot always simultaneously carry the two above-mentioned goals in a fully harmonized and balanced fashion, is provably of less significance than to recognize them both as legitimate aspirations in an age all too easily allocated entirely to one direction or the other. It is because of his insistence on Serbian autonomy that Vuk is best remembered today, and probably because of his folksongs (still frequently read and sung), rather than anything else that his memory is most commonly invoked today. Whereas literacy in the West may have had more long-term international materialistic consequences, that of Eastern Europe has continued to provide a bulwark against deracination. Nevertheless, Vuk certainly had some idea that most of the poems in his collections were not entirely natural and spontaneous folk creations, but like Herder and Kopitar he probably also believed folk artists also contributed to the 'essence' of a people. This is a belief that is very reminiscent of Vuk's criticism of 'intellectuals' who had become ignorant of their own people's heritage. In an age in which it is almost taboo to mention such Herderianisms as 'national character' Vuk's fearless invocation of 'national heritage' through song, poetry and prose seems far less objectionable.

The underlying chord tying together all of Vuk's feverish efforts was 'Europe' (the 'West'), with whom he had a classic double approach–avoidance relationship. Serbia's being admitted to Europe and respected by Europe, but also Serbia's being threatened with detribalization by Europe. Europe desired and feared, Europe gratifying and rejecting: these were his dreams and his nightmares that taken together converted his life into more never-ending turmoil than either one alone could well have done. Ultimately, it was what his campaign was all about and what his songs, tales, Bible and dictionaries sought to accomplish. Neither Nebrija nor Gutenberg was fixated by this poignant dilemma. Although Lefin, whom we are soon to encounter, was also entangled by it, Lefin was both less significant overall than Vuk and more defeated by it than Vuk. Vuk, withered leg and all, would simply not be defeated by anyone or anything. He was like a force of nature. He had the sheer intellectual energy and determination of one who had found his calling late in life, the dedication to exhaustiveness and accuracy of one who had learned these attributes at the hands of great and stern (German) masters whom he dared not disappoint. Vuk was even more than a one-man literacy campaign, because not only did his lifework make literacy meaningful to the ordinary 'person-in-the-street', not only did it introduce the greatness of the Serbs to the Austro-Hungarian Empire that might otherwise have simply regarded them as so much expendable frontier-country cannon-fodder, but he prepared the way for both a cultural rapprochement (as well as the more recent geopolitical imbroglio) between Serbs and South Slavs as a whole. Only Nebrija had a similarly all-inclusive dream, and of the two, Nebrija and Vuk, the latter came much closer to fulfilling it than did the former.

Mendl Lefin (1749–1826)

Continuing eastward we come to the final hero of European vernacular literacy: Menakhem Mendl Lefin. Although he was identified with a 'nonstate language' (Yiddish) and although the age of print reached it in conjunction with modern Eastern-Europe Yiddish in the Slavic lands somewhat later even than it had reached Vuk and many of the other Southern Slavic lands, Lefin's story is in its broad outline very similar to that of the other three that we have already examined. He, like each of the others, had to face and overcome the opposition of the 'church' pertaining to his culture: the Jewish Orthodox Rabbinate. Nevertheless it does differ, both in major and in subtle ways, from those of the others because of specific sociohistorical and sociocultural characteristics of that time, place and sociolinguistic context. These differences may help us understand why Lefin alone was essentially defeated by forces aligned against him.

The major obstacle was that Lefin's first major Yiddish book was an unwitting casualty of the ongoing struggle between two Jewish factions of the time: the Maskilim (enlighteners) and the Khasidim (the pious traditionalists). Lefin himself was very much identified with the Maskilim, whose major goal was to bring Western knowledge, culture, lifestyle and civic roles to Jews who were very much still totally surrounded by their own and by co-territorial cultures that were, for the most part, far removed from those of modern Western societies and cultures. As a young Maskil (singular of Maskilim), Lefin had traveled from Satanov, in the Ukraine, to Berlin, to learn modern Western languages (German and French) and natural sciences, as well as to ponder Mendelssohn's views and approaches vis-à-vis fashioning a modern, rational Judaism. Lefin soon recognized that he could not simply copy Mendelssohnian Judaism and transplant it lock, stock and barrel to a setting in which neither a Jewish nor a gentile rennaissance or reformation had as yet transpired. Nor was he interested in any such wholesale transfer, if only because in the East of Europe, Jews were considered a separate people, with a vernacular and a religion of their very own (very much as were Poles, Ukrainians, Finns, etc.). There could be no thought there of turning them into, 'Russians of Moses' persuasion', in a manner that would parallel the German Maskilim's model of adopting the mantle and motto of being no more nor less than 'Germans of Moses' persuasion'. This was not so much a result of Lefin's being more Herderian than was Mendelssohn nor even as a result of any pervasive pro-Slavic philosophical affinity on Lefin's part (in the midst of which Lefin's entire life had thus far transpired), as much as it was due to certain contemporary Jewish influences which Lefin felt he had to counteract if any kind of Jewish modernization (Lefin's ultimate goal) was to make any headway whatsoever. Basically, Lefin strongly believed (as had his revered teacher Mendelssohn before him) that Jews should become accomplished speakers, readers and writers of the local state language. He saw no other logical course for them to take in their own self-interest. But after many disappointing attempts to reach with his enlightened modernizing message via Hebrew, he finally came to the realization that this goal could be attained most effectively only if Yiddish (and their own Eastern Yiddish at that, rather than via the strange Western Yiddish that they also scarcely knew and often strongly disliked). He came to believe, as Vuk did, that Jews needed to be written to in the language that they spoke, full of popular idioms and pithy expressions that would make it not only far better understood but also more easily remembered and acted upon.

Khasidism and Yiddish

Like the Western Maskilim who he had lived among in Berlin, Lefin was unalterably opposed to the 17th century traditionalist ('fundamentalist') revival known as Khasidism. Its adherents were roundly known among Maskilim as obscurantist, ignorant, superstitious and unwashed (and even, originally, as heretics, due to their revisions in the order of prayer and in observances, as well as their insistence on rabbis of their own). This movement had more recently made deep inroads among Jews in the isolated Slavic world and it was particularly noted for its early cultivation of Eastern Yiddish via popular songs, folktales and rabbinic sermons that became immensely widespread in Eastern Yiddish, at a time when the language was also changing rapidly, both linguistically and socioculturally, from its Western Yiddish origins. While it may have been 'natural' for Lefin to try to bring a manner of Jewish rational wisdom to Eastern European Jews in their Yiddish mother tongue, rather than in the Hebrew that they could neither read easily nor understand fully or empathically, the 'maskilim' (also dubbed and self-called 'misnagdim', that is, 'opponents of khasidus'), favored (1) German or Russian for vernacular and vernacular literacy purposes, both of these languages being honorable state languages that represented westernization, rationality and modernization, and (2) continued fealty to Hebrew for all lofty internal Jewish purposes, such as prayer and study of the venerated Hebrew–Aramaic classics and for the mastery of centuries worth of rabbinic intellectual writings. Yiddish was represented in their writings as a nightmarishly corrupt, hideous, impoverished, stunted and limited language, totally unsuited for the modern mind or soul. Thus, in the eyes of the misnagdim, it was not the religious tradition per se that they claimed was offended by Lefin's misguided efforts, nor even rabbinic authority as such, as much as it was decency itself and the basic maskilic goal of enabling Jews to become modern Europeans, gaining thereby the thanks of their respective governments, of their enlightened co-citizens and of the very spirit and the essence of modernity: to be as one with 'Europe' and all that Mendelssohn had devoted his life to!

The defense of Lefin's effort to dignify the vernacular

Lefin's inauspicious sociolinguistic 'iconoclasm' did elicit some defense, notably that by the veteran Hebrew writer and scholar Shmul Bik. He too was a Maskil but his view of Yiddish was not only a positive one but one that remains distinctly modern and even sophisticated in its arguments to this very day, nearly 200 years later. His views bear citation even now, whenever and wherever late-modernizing languages anywhere require defense against attacks from languages that have attained prior recognition and more certain protection. Indeed, even such illustrious languages of the day as English and German, Bik claimed, had once required defense and had benefited from some of the very same arguments that Bik independently arrived at half a millennium later! All languages that only recently are adopted for certain functions, originally seem coarse, quaint and unsuited for those functions. It is only over time that they are rendered as fit as any others by writers and scholars who utilize them in order to express intricate and sophisticated thoughts. Yiddish too would undoubtedly quickly become elegant in accord with such universal experience. To deny it the right and to restrict its ability to do so *ab initio*, was an expression of bias that ill became those who expressed it and who themselves sought to be regarded as objective and rational intellectuals (as well as of rationality in the public arena).

Indeed, although Lefin soon retired from the fray (translating and preparing only a few more biblical volumes before his untimely demise), it quickly became clear that Bik's prognosis had been quite correct. By well before the end of the century in which Lefin had elicited such strong critique and aroused equally stirring defences, Yiddish literature went through a virtual blossoming of new titles, authors, genres in both belletristic as well as in continually more technical scientific and formal nonfiction functions. Lefin's Bible translation had the bad luck of coming on the scene in the very midst of an internecine dispute (the 'war of the languages', it was soon called) that reflected the deep ideological divisions within Lefin's sociocultural circle almost everywhere in Europe. Hebrew too was just then beginning to be modernized for contemporary vernacular functions (after persisting only as a language of classically expressed texts for well over a millennium), a reversal of fortune the likes of which none of the other heroes of literacy had encountered. Hebrew's rival modernization and revernacularization ultimately reached previously unimagined levels of success, even attaining full state protection in Israel little more than a century and a half after Lefin's efforts transpired. The Hebrew development constitutes a story totally diferent from and even better known than the one we have sketched here focused on Yiddish. Why then did we highlight Yiddish here rather than Hebrew? We did so because Lefin's experience provides us with an important lesson that neither Nebrija, Gutenberg nor Vuk teaches as clearly or as fully, namely, that the road to vernacular literacy was not necessarily preordained to be successful, and it was never an easy road at all, even when it *was* ultimately successful (as it soon was also in the case of Yiddish).

Concluding Reflections on the Four Horsemen of European Vernacular Literacy

After all is said and done, the above story of the four horsemen is here mainly intended as a pedagogic device, interesting though this story undoubtedly may be in and of itself. It is a story that spans the continent, the centuries, the socioreligious traditions and the material and ideological contexts out of which European vernacular literacy grew and developed. As in all human stories, it does not pretend to begin at 'the very beginning' of the processes that abetted its subject matter, in order to illuminate their 'ultimate causes' or 'true roots'; nor does it pretend at all to gauge the 'ultimate consequences' of the processes that it chronicles. It also does not seek to create the impression that vernacular literacy could not have come to the fore in Europe without these four protagonists. Nor was the omnipresent religious opposition to the spread of European vernacular literacy particularly retrograde or unthinking. Indeed, the opposition that it reveals, at each of its major sites, was merely a very 'natural' and predictable reaction to a possibly dislocative innovation, real or imagined, on the part of any preexisting establishment. Nevertheless, the Church (or the churches) soon adjusted to popular vernacular literacy and not only learned to utilize it for their own purposes, but even to advance these purposes thereby, doing so beyond any level that had been attained before vernacular literacy took hold. Indeed, vernacular literacy was like a rising tide: it truly lifted all boats. The same tendency toward foot-dragging revealed by the churches was, doubtlessly, initially true, to some extent, of all the other establishments of the time, be they royal or princely authority, government agency, education, commerce, the workplace or simply the dominant styles of amusement and relaxation of the age in which vernacular literacy began to 'break through' and began its own spread and domination.

Actually, the rise of vernacular literacy is part of the very story of the changing daily life of all of Europe, and, accordingly, the attainment of popular vernacular literacy necessarily proceeded at different rates and in accord with different methods and conventions, depending on different local and national social and cultural circumstances, and was even locally and temporarily reversible. It is to a brief examination of some of these very basic underlying local circumstances that we will turn to in the next chapter.

Note

1. There were of course several prerequisites for the emergence of the printing press in addition to alphabetic writing, among them being: interest and capability for technological improvement, availability of paper, screw-based presses and a system for releasing capital to entrepreneurs.

References

Chartier, R. (ed.) (1989) *The Culture of Print: Power and the Uses of Print in Early Modern Europe*. Princeton: Princeton University Press.
Fishman, J.A. (ed.) (1981) Attracting a following to high culture functions for a language of everyday life. *Never say Die! A Thousand Years of Yiddish in Jewish Life and Letters* (pp. 369–394). Mouton: The Hague.
Houston, R.A. (1988) *Literacy in Early Modern Europe: Culture and Education 1500–1800*. London: Longman.
Kloss, H. (1952) *Die Entwicklung neuer germanischer Kultersprachen von 1800 bis 1950*, (1). Munich: Pohl.
Man, J. (2002) *Gutenberg: How One Man Remade the World*. New York: John Wiley.
Weinreich, M. 1980 (1973) *History of the Yiddish Language* (S. Noble and J.A. Fishman, trans.). Chicago: University of Chicago Press (equals Vols. 1–2 of the 4 volume Yiddish original, 1973).

Chapter 6
Micro-factors in the Societal Spread of Vernacular Literacy

If, as many have intimated before, vernacular literacy was 'a miracle waiting to happen', how then, that is, by what means or along which paths, did this miracle's wondrous ways proceed to unfold? As we have already noted, there were many large-scale interregional-European differences that played a part in that spread (Chapter 4). Certainly, human agency was everywhere involved and certain representatives can be selected to illuminate various facets, challenges and means of the rise of vernacular literacy (Chapter 5). But between the above two extremely different (but inseparable) levels of analysis, we are still left to inquire as to the interstitial processes that tie the two of them together. Micro-processes are interstitial in that they reveal the lower-order, smaller scale underpinnings that are necessarily involved in all continent-wide as well as subcontinental regional differences in literacy rates. Although smaller in scale than the factors that are operative at the regional or sectional level, the micro-process factors are also not as fine-grained as those that pertain to the detailed individual biographical level. The current chapter cannot trace (or even suggest) all such interstitial or underlying variables at the microlevel, but the few that we have chosen to examine below are, hopefully, among the most significant of them all. Even so, we can only touch upon them briefly.

Elitist Literacy and Its Outgrowths

Let us take care to begin 'with the right foot'. There was literacy aplenty in Europe even before there was vernacular literacy of any kind or generality at all. There was hardly a place in Europe in which the elites of the state, of the church(es), of the schools and even among the gentry and leaders of commerce and industry, were not themselves either literate or employers of scribes and clerks on their own behalf by the 15th century.

Albeit that the texts and copy that were then produced were hand-lettered and recorded on some variety of parchment or velum, their omnipresence is a sufficient indication that literacy per se was widely recognized, valued and rewarded or honored and put to use, even among many of those of power, stature and renown who could not quite evince literacy themselves (beyond the rudiments of a signature). Indeed, from the very earliest times, European elites kept or commissioned the keeping of records for reasons of state, of worship, of study, of business, of entertainment and of personal vanity. Increasingly, the coming of popular vernacular literacy involved very great changes in the incidence and in the class structure of the participants in a variety of literacy processes and scenarios, and, accordingly, also in the rendering of the texts themselves and in their means of enactment and distribution, as well as, ultimately, participating in the costs of their preparation, ownership, display and conservation. However, each such extension had consequences of its own and, collectively, they made texts become vital parts of the lives of a totally unprecedented number and variety of individuals.

Social and cultural factors in fostering the spread of literacy into non-elitist circles

A well-attested characteristic feature of European sociocultural reality is the endless continuum of ties that existed between its elites and others of lesser standing in the secular or in the religious order. The flow of contacts and influences between the secular and the clerical orders existed at every level, between middle level elites, lower level elites, fully qualified craftsmen and prosperous burgers, ordinary city dwellers and countryside squires. There was often a fairly constant contact and interaction that did not cease by any means at the city line. Although the barriers and borders between these subgroups were highly variable from place to place and from time to time, the flow of ideas, styles and even artifacts across these social borders was considerable relative to many parts of the world. This porous between-class quality of many European social arrangements made the top-down flow of influence and innovation (called 'gesunkenes Kulturgut' in discussions of the spread of folkloric material) a major fact of life insofar as the spread of literacy was concerned. Both active top-down spread and more passive top-down seepage need to be recognized in this connection. This was not inevitable, nor everywhere, nor always so, but to a very appreciable extent every social class acquired vernacular literacy substantially from its 'betters', who both aided and abetted it and often felt obliged to do so (i.e. to be change agents) from a variety of mixed motives. Parent–child, religious–secular, master–servant (or apprentice), tutor–student interactions are so frequently mentioned in local letters, diaries and accounts, that they may be deemed an ongoing and accelerating urban sociocultural feature, rather than merely an individual act of 'Christian kindness', or a relationship of personal convenience, or even an arrangement from which the grantor stands to gain more than the grantee.

Top-down transfers of skill and empowerment

With the advent of vernacular literacy, the top-down transfer of skill and empowerment required even less (1) downwardly directed initiative or (2) special-purpose between-class arrangements. Both (1) and (2) became much more commonplace than they had been when classical literacy was still in vogue or when the earliest periods of vernacular literacy had just begun. Even the early vernacular literacy movements in Eastern Europe often began as exemplary top-down efforts on the part of a few dedicated and exceptional pioneers and risk takers. When vernacular literacy jumped across the Atlantic, it also began as a top-down social custom for the betterment of fortunate but hitherto underprivileged individuals and communities (albeit along mostly within-racial lines).

Entrepreneurship

However, the importance of within-class upward self-improvement motives in the spread of literacy in general and of vernacular literacy in particular also cannot be overestimated. Such motives are not always operative everywhere, nor were they always operative in Europe. However, from around the beginning of the 15th century, Europe went through a series of interlocked cultural, intellectual and scientific changes that made the acquisition and dissemination of literacy more advantageous to all concerned than it might have been otherwise and elsewhere. The discovery of the New World and the resulting race for colonies, the industrial revolution, the expansion of urban life, the commercial revolution, the land-transportation revolution and the vast improvements in public health, education and welfare generally preceded and interacted reciprocally with the spread of numeracy, social mobility and of vernacular literacy most particularly. Working one's way up and out of one's family of procreation and on to the social mobility ladder was greatly assisted by the acquisition of more ample literacy as well as by the acquisition of the contacts, venture capital, skills and information that literacy facilitated. Each one of our 'heroes of literacy' was (had to be) an entrepreneur, a competitor and a recipient of public or of charitable funds. Gutenberg's seminal invention of moveable type, the printing press, his experiments with paper, ink, type faces and beautification of the printed page all reflect the spirit of inquiry and of activity that both fostered literacy and was fostered by it. A variety of ideological developments are often both predecessors and consequences of changes in the material realm.

A 'Chicken and Egg' Problem

Material progress, intellectual progress and ideological developments have frequently been closely interwoven, and so it was in connection with the vernacular literacy nexus as well. The democratic impulse promoted by vernacular literacy could not be contained as easily as it could during the days of classical literacy, vernacular literacy immediately implied shared literacy, that is, literacy as an entitlement for one and all. When the view became widespread that an ordinary male burger should both read and write and that it was acceptable to do so roughly as one spoke, that further promoted contact and continuity between all segments of society, even women and members of 'nonstate-forming minorities regarded as indigenous'. Democratic sentiments also more easily spread among the national liberation movements among these very minorities, even in connection with their different nonstate-forming languages, and even regardless of whether ethnic separation, autonomy and independence were being pursued. None of the latter could have arisen without vernacular literacy based on some degree of intervarietal standardization. The latter became possible only because of the standardization experiences of the state vernacular that preceded them. 'Write as you speak' had always been a 'more or less' affair and varieties judged to be more discrepant from their respective mainstream standardizations often only came to be recognized for the purpose of a standardization of 'their own' vernaculars later than did those considered less discrepant. This process will probably continue fairly endlessly, whenever different local identities are also strongly held. All such accommodations are motivated by varieties of the same democratic sentiments and convictions that supported mainstream vernacular literacy to begin with (even if lesser gains in upward social mobility result therefrom). Vernacular literacy generally involves both liberating and constricting features. The expanse of territory over which vernacular literacy holds sway may very well be less than that which was formerly included within the sway of the classical that it attempts to displace. On the other hand, the sheer size of the potential audience that vernacular literacy enfranchises may well be ever so much greater than that of more prestigious classical literacy (and is usually also accompanied by an ethnic-identity liberation claim). In an age and atmosphere in which democratic populism trumps classical sophistication, the latter inevitably takes second place to the former and is considered to be a victory for the greater good.

The Elephant in the Room: The Growth in Parsimonious Communicational Possibilities

At roughly the same time and in roughly the same areas in which vernacular literacy began to grow, there occurred an expansion in the reach of the instrumentalities of communication. The number of cities grew greatly and increased the average propinquity among inhabitants of the land. In addition, of course, the means of intraurban and interurban communication increased as roads both increased and improved. Roads became major avenues of the spread of information of all kinds (including literacy and second language learning). A similar expansion also occurred in connection with sea (and, ultimately, air) communication. Sea-borne channels of communication brought European vernacular literacy to the New World, Africa and Asia. No colonizers, settlers or conquerors brought a classical tongue out of Europe as a general medium of writing and reading. Letters to and from Europe were almost always in the vernacular, as was the lion's share of all printed materials.

Of all of the several causes and avenues of the spread of vernacular literacy, none have been more documented nor more documentable than those pertaining to the growth of methods and means of communication. It is as a result of such counts made in various locales and over a span of centuries that it can be fully proven that cities were centers of literacy before less concentrated settlements and far earlier than was the rural and semi-rural countryside. Cities had business establishments, schools and, in the long run, also churches and governmental offices that both required and supported vernacular literacy. Men normally became vernacularly literate more rapidly than did women, primarily due to the gender bias that was long so prevalent in all of the institutions of work or learning in which literacy could be conveyed by design. Upper- and middle-class persons became vernacularly literate before did persons of lower-class standing, the younger did on the whole before the older, Jews and Christians earlier than did Moslems and 'heathens'. Many of the foregoing factors are themselves overlapping and even redundant insofar as explaining differences in the rate of vernacular literacy acquisition is concerned. Furthermore, these several factors continue to be important outside of Europe as well as within it, as well as among those who acquired vernacular literacy in non-Latin alphabets, as well as among those who acquired it in a large number of different Latin type faces. While it would be false to claim that vernacular literacy 'spread by contagion', to the extent that both require close contact, both depended upon similar societal arrangements. Vernacular literacy in Europe was simply too advantageous to those who controlled it for it to be long kept under wraps there given its relatively porous and interactive conventions.

Summary

All in all, and by way of summary, the spread of vernacular literacy in Europe proceeded in accord with the ways and means of the spread of social change more generally, when compared with the diffusion of innovations of almost any kind. The spread of vernacular literacy was an innovation, indeed, it was a triple innovation in conjunction with all three of its components (spread, vernacular and literacy) and one that also coincided with, was assisted by and itself supported other innovations prompting social change. But in some respects, the spread of vernacular literacy was also *sui generis*. The world was never the same again once Gutenberg timidly entered into the arena of vernacular publication. However, vernacular literacy in Europe is not something about which it can be said that it was a foregone conclusion that it would succeed. As there is in every case of attempted innovation, there was resistance as well. Printers were driven out of one medieval university town after the professors accused them of being in league with the devil because they were placing God's word into improper hands. Scribes and purveyors were certainly resistant. It is no accident that each of our four horsemen of vernacular literacy so frequently practiced the arts of flattery to some extent at least. They probably could not have 'made it' otherwise and, even so, Gutenberg died quite penniless for all of his blood, sweat, tears and inventiveness. Even today, many newspapers and journals have had to cease publication or are on the very verge of bankruptcy. All innovations must cope with subsequent innovations that can overtake and displace them. That too is part and parcel of the ongoing story of social change. Those who live by social change are also at risk of dying by the same processes that had previously brought them into being.

The future of vernacular literacy will ultimately depend on its utility in the advancement of knowledge, social status and expertise. Thus far, the telephone, radio, television or newfangled handheld electronic devices have unseated it on a widespread basis. Only time will tell whether even newer devices relying primarily on spoken or other nonprint communication and retrieval will continue to share the vernacular turf with literacy. Somewhere in Africa and Asia, farmers and newly urbanized folk are being ushered from illiteracy straight through to digital communication. Will this then become a major avenue of education and social mobility for the hitherto underprivileged, while literacy as we know it today will become the property of restricted and selected social circles (akin to what happened to classical literacy centuries ago)? The future centrality of vernacular literacy depends on the eventual outcome of this momentous contest and generally unrecognized struggle that is just beginning and that will play itself out during the lifetime of our grandchildren.

References

Deutsch, K.W. (1943) The trend of European Nationalism: The language aspect. *American Political Science Review* 36 (1942), 533–541.

Kloss, H. and McConnell, G.D. (eds) (1978) *The Written Languages of the World: A Survey*. Quebec City: Laval University Press.

Sarton, G. (Vol. 1, 1927); (Vol. 2, 1931); (Vol. 3, 1953) *Introduction to the History of Science*. Baltimore: Carnegie Institute.

Chapter 7
The 'Literacy Bullies on the Block'

Thus far, we have said practically nothing at all about two of the major and oldest languages of European vernacular literacy: English and French. We have 'saved the best for last', so that with all their similarity to the processes and lines of development that characterize vernacular literacy elsewhere in Europe, we could better appreciate their distinctiveness (if any) in fostering vernacular literacy around the world (and particularly in their own former and current colonies). The European Union's (EU) policy of recognizing the state languages of all of its member states, and even some of their minority languages, for the purposes of presentations to the Union's parliament, and UNO's policy of recognizing English, French, Spanish, Russian, Chinese and Arabic for parliamentary discussion, only serves to disguise from the unknowing that the only major languages of both are English and French and that of these two, English is the one that is on top (functionally, both in speech and in writing, if not statutorily). Indeed, the latter organization's International Court of Justice recognizes only English and French.

Since excellent specialized volumes have long been available about the routes to vernacular literacy traveled by English and French, we will content ourselves in this chapter to briefly reviewing their current policies in former colonies and continued spheres of political, economic and cultural affairs. In both cases the spread of local vernacular adult literacy is resisted, in the Anglosphere by foot-dragging and in the Francosphere by stonewalling. The differences between them are both greater and more instructive than is ordinarily apparent.

The Exportation of English Literacy and of Indigenous Vernacular Literacy to the Anglosphere

We can assume that English would be the favored language of 'exoliteracy' in the Anglosphere, and for two telling reasons: (1) because of the residual (but often quite tangible) benefits with which Anglo-literacy is associated in those settings and (2) because of its worldwide prominence or predominance in economic, educational, diplomatic and technological or scientific realms. As a result of this very small number of predictors, there are only four possible outcomes, namely (a) former colonies in which English is clearly dominant relative to the (other) local vernaculars, (b) countries in which it is co-official with one or more local vernaculars but where such power sharing is purely ceremonial or pro-forma, (c) countries in which the sharing of power with one or more local vernaculars is both substantial and well protected, and, finally, (d) countries in which English has essentially been displaced from dominance and still lingers on, more in recognition of past glories or as an option for second or third language instruction, than as a vehicle of major current behavioral or attitudinal societal functions. Let us start with (d), above, and work our way backwards, going from the least to the most exclusive role of English.

Polities in the Anglosphere in which English has been almost completely marginalized

Strange as it may seem to most confirmed Anglophones, there are a few instances of such situations. Perhaps the most dramatic example of this kind is the Atlantic coast of Costa Rica, where a variety of pidgin English developed among former slaves imported from Africa and became intergenerationally continuous roughly a hundred or more years ago. Not only did support for vernacular literacy not develop in this pidgin or in any other variety related to it, but the pidgin itself has continued to shrink significantly during the past decade or so and may well disappear in a few more, as Costa Rica develops economically and as racist attitudes weaken sufficiently to admit this population into fully hispanicized citizenry. Of course, it is easy to dismiss this example on the grounds that it 'merely' deals with a pidgin variety of English but pidgins cannot and should not be so easily dismissed. There are other varieties of pidgin English around the world that either continue their independent existence as such (e.g. in parts of Cameroon, Nigeria and elsewhere). Some have even developed literacy functions and standards of their own. Indeed, some African varieties of pidgin English not only continue to be strong today but are even making headway (although not necessarily in literacy functions) relative to other surrounding African languages and even in comparison to English itself. When and if such pidgins cease to exist their erstwhile speakers often enter into identities that might lead them more assuredly toward one indigenous literacy or another. But even this is not always the outcome for struggling pidgin, since there is ample support for the view that the spread of one pidgin can be best counteracted by the spread of another. In many cases, of course, vernacular literacy may not be involved or in the offing in either context.

Settings in which the 'sharing' of English's formerly exclusive power with one or more local vernaculars is now both substantial and well protected

Both Francosphere Canada and Anglosphere Puerto Rico provide examples of the substantial retreat of English in the politicized contexts of competition with other languages of vernacular literacy. The most that English can currently hope for in both of the foregoing settings is that it may remain or become a more or less easily accessed language of co-literacy for populations whose spoken vernaculars and routes to vernacular literacy are either via French or Spanish. Even this severely compromised solution for the English literacy that was formerly clearly in control is by no means assured, either because the competing language is successfully attracting higher and higher proportions of individuals among those populations that attain literacy at all, or because literacy per se is often of sufficiently questionable utility that co-literacy becomes an unnecessary and useless luxury. Legally, however, constitutional guarantees are currently observed that protect a role for English in education and in government and in public services for defined classes of individuals that want or need them in English. In both Quebec and Puerto Rico, the English-literate are a distinct minority but still a large enough and certainly an influential enough subgroup of the local populations that they have been afforded or have demanded historical privileges that they might not be accorded elsewhere or otherwise. Both of these settings reflect a change in the balance of power, so that a previously defeated and subjugated population has come into a degree of political power and has, accordingly, visited this reversal of power on the former masters. Literacy functions, like all societal functions of languages no matter how long they have been implemented, reflect facts (or at least opportunities) 'on the ground', rather than any presumed natural order of things. Although all Puerto Ricans become biliterate in both Spanish and English, the quality and degree of their English literacy is both low and has been falling for half a century or more. Even the spoken and sung English and that the major mass-communication media inevitably utilize and that the reverse migrants from the mainland have introduced into popular Puerto Rican Spanish usage has not compensated for the loss in functional and functioning English literacy in all but a thin upper crust. This class has not developed into a counterpart to the hereditary 'Anglo Indians' in India, because its appearance is both too recent and also too foreign in origin, but, given another half century of continuity, that too may yet come to pass. The marginalization of English in Puerto Rico is one factor that has rendered US statehood very unlikely (if not impossible) for Puerto Rico, even though its citizens have all or almost all of the other rights and obligations of mainland US citizens, including armed services duty during national emergencies. Although Puerto Rico is known as 'la colonia perfumada' to its fully independent Latin American neighbors, its exceptional status is indicated by its being the only part of the United States in which the vast majority of citizens are neither functionally English literate nor even English speaking on a regular daily basis. Finally, it must be noted that the situation of literacy in Puerto Rico does not directly influence that of Spanish on the mainland, where for all its millions of speakers, Spanish literacy is far weaker (as in the next case below). Although Hispanics have been in the border-region from even before their incorporation into the United States, most of them are widely perceived as unwanted immigrants and, as such, they are 'low man on the totem-pole' insofar as language rights are concerned in many localities. Amerindians, on the other hand, often benefit from 'first nation' status but even when this provides some support for child-vernacular literacy their languages have undergone such attrition among adults that vernacular literacy is rarely a serious or a reachable goal for them at all.[1]

Settings in which English is co-official with one or more local vernaculars but where such power sharing is often more ceremonial or pro-forma and limited to a small upper crust of society (particularly insofar as literacy is concerned)

Despite many superficial similarities, the differences between English literacy in Puerto Rico and English literacy in India can be attributed to the fact that India is a fully independent polity made up of numerous vernaculars some of which have long been associated with literacies of their own. Indeed, although the pursuit of English literacy remains a matter of real and official national interest in India, English is not situated in a territorial entity (State or Province) of its own and, therefore, being 'everyone's baby', it is also no one's 'dearest child'.

The 'outsourcing' feature of America's industrial prowess and several recent media and Broadway 'sensations' have made the entire world aware of the large numbers of individuals literate in English among the half-billion people of India. However, in a country of such demographic proportions, even as many as 25 million English literates (and there are probably not anywhere near that many who are such at a truly functional level) are but as a drop in the bucket.

Notwithstanding the many illustrious Anglo-Indians in the country's recent past (foremost among them the members of the Nehru dynastic family), and notwithstanding the many first rate English journals and newspapers that are available in most parts of the country (some with circulations that would be the envy of most English media in the United States or England), the true relative nonprominence of English in the nationwide life of India is probably better reflected in the proportion of vernacular films among all of the films annually produced in India. The prominence of English-in-print is probably greater than it is in films, because of the greater employment and business opportunities associated with English, but it is still dwarfed by the total mass of print in Indian vernaculars, up to and including the higher levels of books, encyclopedias and reference materials intended for any larger general audience. English literacy is essential for India's specialists in economic growth and political outreach, but for a billion or so common folk, it is just another language in the huge world of endless, inaccessible and often bewildering world dialects, languages and scripts.

Also of this type, but with an even less crucial role as to reliance on English literacy for world outreach, is the situation of such literacy in Francophone Canada outside of Montreal. The difference in favor of French literacy is largely due to its demographic magnitude relative to all other co-present languages, its now secure historical and constitutional position as a co-founding language with its own financial resources and linguistic standardization, and, above all, the international prestige and might of its French 'protector', against roughshod English dominance. Of course, in neither Anglophone nor Francophone Canada has Native American (Indian or Eskimo [Inuit]) literacy been firmly or intergenerationally established.

The situation of local vernacular literacies in the Republic of South Africa, in which 11 languages are co-official, is in most cases substantially more precarious than is that of French in Canada outside of Quebec. The major differences are demographic and the profound absence of any local language that is anywhere near as useful as is French in Anglophone Canada. Neville Alexander, a Black South African scholar and passionate advocate of African languages' development and literacy, realized, while serving a 10-year sentence on Robben Island for alleged sabotage during the antiapartheid struggle, among other things, that literacy in the indigenous languages of the continent is indispensable for economic development, political democracy and cultural dignity. But among the 'co-officials', only Afrikaans has a substantial number of literate speakers, many of them Black, some of the latter having acquired the language as their mother tongue rather than later in school. There is still a chance (far from a certainty) that Afrikaans' recent decline, since the independence of the Republic of South Africa was attained, can be reversed, but if this is so, it is partially due to the enhanced status accorded to the many Bantu languages that have also been granted 'co-official' status. Efforts to develop biliteracy involving indigenous African languages, however, have yet to gain momentum, although the Western Cape Education Department has now started to implement bilingual education programmes in the first six years of schooling. For those who take a more pessimistic view of developments, a good rule of thumb may be that whenever a country has more than three to four 'official' languages, most of them are for window-dressing purposes, rather than for serious functional use in the allocation of power. India is the major exception to this rule, but its multiliteracy is of a deeply historical nature and reinforced largely from non-Western (largely Buddhist and Islamic) traditions that were generally already well established before the Raj began and that are generally non-exportable. Overall, English can hardly be said to have covered itself with glory in the pursuit of vernacular literacies in the lands that it conquered in earlier centuries.

Former colonies in which English is clearly dominant, as compared to the local vernaculars (in most of which only minimal literacy is cultivated if any at all)

Finally, we must at least mention that there are two major overseas English mother-tongue countries (the United States and Australia) in which English literacy is practically the only one to be seriously cultivated beyond the level of childhood literacy, whether publicly or privately. If in connection with settings of type (b) we said 'overall, English can hardly be said to have covered itself with glory in the pursuit of vernacular literacies in the lands that it conquered in earlier centuries', this is doubly and triply so in the settings of type (a), where whatever societally based literacies other than English that are still encountered are either restricted to early childhood moribund or recent immigrant based. This is hardly a record for a champion of immigrants and of sociolinguistic justice to be proud of.

A Brief Comparison with Vernacular Literacies in the Francophone Sphere

The constancy of transplanted European political and cultural patterns is starkly and dramatically revealed by comparing the Anglosphere's and the Francosphere's attitudes and policies toward vernacular literacies. Another way of grasping this same phenomenon is to compare the processes of devolution and of accommodation to local indigenous vernacular literacies in Great Britain itself with the continued centralization of French political and cultural policy and its continued policy of rejection, dismissal and blockage vis-à-vis nonmainstream vernacular literacies in metropolitan France. The latter approach has continued, even though it can no longer be pretended (as was formerly the case before independence was reluctantly granted to them after World War II) that the countries of the Francosphere are just ordinary departments of France itself on the continent per se as a result of these radically different points of departure toward vernacular literacies in the 'mother countries' themselves. There are proportionally more examples of type (c) and (d) accommodations to vernacular literacies in the Anglosphere and more of type (a) and (b) accommodations in the Francosphere, although the 'Loi Toubon' (Law no. 94–665 of 4 August 1994) is more or less a dead letter in France itself insofar as the protection of French and French alone in France itself (it is now quite acceptable (in most social circles there) to refer to e-mail as 'e-mail'). Although that Loi was never applied as assiduously overseas as in the mother country, the governmental departments and agencies supporting the original policy of Francophonie all over the Francophone sphere are still 'carrying on' as in the days of yore, as separate, ongoing and eternal features of 'French national radiance'.

Outside of the Moslem Maghreb, there are no settings in the Francosphere in which French literacy has been substantially marginalized or has become even partially secondary (as has occurred with English literacy on the Costa Rican Caribbean coast and in Puerto Rico, or even as has occurred in India or in the Philippines or in Tanzania). Conversely, with the exception of French Canada, there is no Francosphere country (certainly, no major Francosphere county) in which French has become the dominant spoken language of almost all of its citizens and well nigh the only language of literacy of its huge population (almost equaling en toto that of France itself). There have been some significant recent exceptions, such as the development of bilingual education initiatives (pédagogie convergente) in Mali (Rassool, 2008). More typical, by far, however, is the position of local literacies in Niger, Senegal, Burkina Faso, Mozambique, Côte d'Ivoire, Gabon (and on, and on, and on throughout the Francophone world not to mention separately the various pidgin areas within Francosphere countries), where no local vernacular literacies at all are or have ever been governmentally cultivated, recognized or supported. It is noteworthy that the Church conducted and supported vernacular literacy efforts for adults conducted by a few (mostly Protestant and/or Linguistic Summer Institute [LSI] in nature) Western-affiliated church organizations in these countries. Although the efforts of these institutions have been Herculean (involving the creation and revision of writing systems, including tonal and vowel length notations), their curricula are essentially restricted to vernacular translations of the New Testament and/or a small selection of prayers.

Even so, they are closely watched by government agencies, which are not above counting the adult students attending these schools in order to inflate their own national adult literacy rates, to make sure that they do not stray into secular areas or topics. At the same time, government-sponsored adult literacy efforts (devoted exclusively to French) are very lightly attended and suffer from very high dropout rates, even though they do not lack for funds, materials or teachers, all of which the church-schools often lack. This is not to deny that literacy of any kind is often looked upon as a foreign, useless and often disturbing or antagonistic skill among populations marked by great poverty and lack of food, clothing and shelter. For such populations it is not altogether clear whether even vernacular literacy would be the most immediately effective step toward the immediate solution of pressing problems. On the other hand, in the absence of massive employment opportunities under government auspices, exoglossic literacy suffers from the very same liabilities that still may surround vernacular literacy in impoverished settings, be they in Africa or elsewhere. Literacy (including vernacular literacy) is not a cure-all for all the ills of humanity, notwithstanding the enthusiasm and promises that have, at times, been mustered in connection with it.[2]

Other European Vernaculars as Competitors with Local Vernacular Literacies Elsewhere

All in all, we can find examples of decline, growth and even of linguagenesis in the Anglosphere and Francosphere ex-colonial world insofar as local vernacular literacies are involved. Taken all in all, the co-occurrence of all of these developments is an indication that the spread of European vernacular literacy has neither receded nor run out of steam outside of its original continental confines. The roles of other European Vernaculars, when exported abroad as languages of conquerors, colonists or settlers (above and beyond English and French) reveal pretty much the same picture. These 'other languages' (Dutch, Italian, Portuguese, Spanish, German and Swedish) have each held sway over non-European territories, for varying periods of time in the past. Dutch, German, Italian and Swedish have entirely retreated by now, except for a few remaining extraterritorial dreamers and sycophants (e.g. the 'last defenders of Dutch in Aruba and Curacao', who oppose Papiamento and staunchly defend Dutch there, so that one or two local children can qualify for the very few competitive annual scholarships awarded to those who attend high school in Dutch). In actuality, this leaves only Spanish and Portuguese as the last European holdouts, for us to examine in competition with local vernacular literacies.

The position of Spanish abroad is often not thought of in connection with foreign rule, because its once mind-boggling holdings in the Americas have, except for Puerto Rico, all attained independence. Nevertheless, this still leaves open for examination the language policies of this former 'great empire' in the few 'straggler colonies' that remain on continents outside of Europe to this very day. Spanish has been exceedingly resistant to the local vernaculars wherever it is politically ascendant (as in Africa), on the one hand, as well as very eager to attain local recognition, where it is not (as on the US mainland). In Latin America, out of the many hundreds of native languages that existed before the arrival of the Conquistadores, only varieties of Guarani (in Paraguay) and the Quechua/Quichua (in and around Ecuador/Peru) have survived and have attained and maintained weak and modest degrees of vernacular literacy. In the United States, Spanish has become the foremost (and still growing) minority tongue and has attained administrative recognition in New Mexico and Puerto Rico (in both of which Spanish is co-official) and civil-rights recognition (for voting and all government-related services) everywhere else, that is, even in those states in which English has ostensibly been declared the 'Official Language'.

All in all, the difference between 'Spanish as giver or grantor' and 'Spanish as receiver' of vernacular literacy is marked. This also applies to Spanish Africa (Sahara), where no nonnative literacies whatsoever are recognized (with the possible partial exception of Arabic). Thus Spanish provides a noteworthy countercase to the generalization that colonial policies toward local vernacular literacies are commonly little more than transplantations of the policy approaches applied to minority vernacular literacies in their European ('metropolitan') heartlands. The liberalization of vernacular literacy policy that has ultimately permitted separate Basque, Catalan, Gallego and even Asturian literacies was never applied in the

Spanish colonies abroad. In its 'at home' policies, Spain, vis-à-vis minority vernacular literacies, is permissive, similar to Great Britain's treatment of Welsh, Irish and Scots; in its overseas policies, Spain is similar to France's repressive treatment of the vernaculars of Mali, Gabon and Niger.

Portuguese remains as a colonial language today only in huge Angola and Mozambique, in tiny Goa, as well as in several other even tinier island possessions. Important initiatives in bilingual education involving Portuguese and several indigenous languages are currently taking place in Mozambique. For the most part, however, overseas vernacular literacy possibilities have been totally ignored or suppressed. Cape Verdean has been recognized by the United States for the purposes of Bilingual Education (for Cape Verdean children in and around Massachusetts), but that vernacular language has obtained no such (nor any other vernacular-related) recognition in Cape Verde itself during the half-millennium when it was under Portuguese control.

On the whole, the record of former and current European colonizers vis-à-vis the encouragement and recognition of vernacular literacy aspirations and attainments in their overseas and offshore locations is, clearly, hardly a distinguished one.[3] The situation is slightly better in the British and Anglo-American spheres since the end of World War II. Nevertheless, the needs of most indigenous peoples have been neglected for so long that hardly any of them can be expected to either survive or recover as instruments of general societal use. This, and the disdainful French (and other colonializing European) complicity and counterpart to it, should be clearly kept in mind when they come to be increasingly rivaled and inevitably replaced by vernaculars that were once dismissively looked down upon as unworthy carriers of power and, therefore, of sophistication and of elegance as well (not to speak of modernization). It will be a Hobson's choice as to whether 'Sic transit gloria mundi' or 'Sic semper tyrannis' will be the ultimate verdict that humanity as a whole will ultimately pronounce upon them. Perhaps 'Sic eunt fata lingum' (thus go the fates of languages), would be the most appropriate comment of all, because their replacements too will suffer similar triumphs, penalties and verdicts once the sun sets on their own inevitably passing but once seemingly 'everlasting places in the sun'.

Notes

1. Tanzania is another major setting that exhibits most of the characteristics of (b) (see p. 76) with respect to its allocation of functions to English and Swahili, particularly insofar as literacy is concerned.

2. Perhaps note should be taken here of Father Maurice Oudet's remark about the internet in Burkina Faso to the effect that 'more and more farmers know how to read and write in their own language ... but there is nothing for them to read there because information that would be useful to them is printed in French' (1999, cited in Omoniyi 2003). Thus it is that one country's 'eternal radiance' comes at the cost of another's starving poor.
3. The introduction or permission regarding vernacular literacy granted to Kurdish in Turkey and in nearby Kurdish areas in Iraq should also be noted, albeit that they are primarily a result of Turkey's recent pursuit of EU admission and of anti-Iraqi-warfare designs.

Reference

Rassool, N. (2008) *Global Issues in Language, Education and Development: Perspectives from Postcolonial Countries.* Clevedon: Multilingual Matters.

Chapter 8
Vernacular Literacy for What?

Nebrija championed a Spanish vernacular literacy yet-to-come for the greater glory of the new empire that Spain was destined to govern overseas. Gutenberg may simply have wanted to bring literacy to the common folk of his time. Vuk may have wanted to free such folk from the yoke of the Church and to gain the respect of Europe for the Serbian language. Lefin wanted to attain the blessings of modernization for the masses whom he thought to be backward and superstitious. Most of those who have labored in the vineyards of vernacular literacy during the past half-millennium have had some such vision of a greater good in mind, but the question still remains as to whether any of our heros really succeeded and if one did so more than another. These are actually extremely hard questions to answer with any degree of accuracy (since we have no common metric for success that could enable us to compare four different goals such as the foregoing). Even such a perspectival question as whether one hero believed that he had succeeded more so than did the others is factually unanswerable, simply because the historical record does not provide data comparing the perspectives of individuals who lived centuries apart and lacked a common language. One thing seems clearer, however, namely that vernacular literacy per se is usually merely an intermediary goal along the road to something other and greater than itself, something which (it is hoped [by its advocates]) literacy would enable the literate to attain more than it is possible for the illiterate to do so.

Vernacular literacy functions within a hierarchy of goals, such that each one is followed by yet another that is even greater, more abstract, more elusive than the one before it. Vernacular literacy is part of 'the impossible dream', dreams which remain vital to human progress, even as it is necessary to go beyond them to an even more encompassing (and impossible) level of verifiable attainment. Humanity's 'reach must exceed its grasp, or what's a heaven for?' Partial failures are a foregone conclusion in any such pursuits, but they do not make the efforts themselves worthless. Far from it. Such partially failed efforts help us understand the true complexity of society, culture and social planning as a whole. They hold out the promise of achieving approximations to ultimate goals, even if the approximations are only asymptotically productive, getting closer and closer but never actually getting 'all the way there'. There are a number of such 'illustrious failures' which have, indeed, dignified our lives, as individuals, as collectivities and as a species. Failures such as these actually keep hope alive.

A number of often mentioned outcomes of the pursuit of literacy are such pious verities as:

(a) Advancement of human well-being (health, education, welfare, social attainment and social mobility).
(b) Advancement of religion in general.
(c) Advancement of a particular religion or denomination.
(d) Advancement of democratic participation in government and in society more generally.
(e) Advancement in communication, innovation, art, the sciences, the humanities and in orientation to human history and to the cosmos as a whole.
(f) Advancement in the attainment of a more self-accepting, other-accepting and reflective and nonjudgmental life.
(g) Advancement of responsible citizenship, environmental responsibility and biodiversity.
(h) Advancement of higher levels of functioning in all cognitive, emotional and interpersonal realms.
(i) Attainment of the greatest good, for the greatest number in connection with the greatest number and variety of human attributes.

The above list can be expanded fairly endlessly, which is not to say that agreement can be attained as to the precise meanings of all of its terms, much less as to the criteria of their degrees of attainment. If we are still some distance away from adequately documenting the degree of attainment of vernacular literacy per se, even for the present (not to mention for precious points during the past of different segments of humanity), it is quite clear that we are a long, long way away from achieving much closure with respect to documenting even the perspectival attainment of the higher level goals of vernacular literacy. However such philosophical and empirical quests are not will-o'-the-wisps. They are important theoretical and empirical desiderata.

The Road to Heaven is Littered with Good Intentions

Unfortunately, this is not likely to be a gratifying pursuit insofar as the adherents of vernacular literacy are concerned. There has never before been a period of human history with as high an incidence of vernacular literacy as our own. Nevertheless, ours has been an age of holocausts, planned mass starvations and other decimations and rank injustices (all perpetrated by some of the most vernacular literacy-advanced societies the world has ever known). How can this come to pass? Apparently, the growth in the attainment of vernacular literacy efforts can and does occur simultaneously with the attainment of the growth in capacity to initiate and conduct other massively conducted authoritative efforts of a far less savory kind. Any multilayered and multivariate study will reveal such unanticipated side effects. Thus, the future of complex social research (and of interventions on behalf of humanity more generally) lies in the support attained by societal abilities to emphasize the positive and eliminate the negative. Via instituting yet other programs and projects, together with and alongside of the pursuit of vernacular literacy, the long road ahead for social policy in this crucial area will become more constructively traveled and more conclusively researchable. We must not throw out the vernacular-literacy-baby with the negative side-effects-bathwater.

With respect to its more proximate effects, vernacular literacy has attained a fantastic record, almost regardless of the language, script or immediate reward system involved. The few exceptions to this rule generally pertain to clashes between two reward systems and their respective associated languages and literacies. Obviously, the stronger of the two wins and the weaker loses (unless some other accommodation between the two is reached, whenever no zero-sum game is involved and both sides can win, as with Samnorsk ('unified Norwegian') and Riksmal ('government Norwegian') in Norway). Indeed, this is precisely the arena in which language planning in general and corpus planning in particular have achieved their most marked successes and have rendered language planning in general into one of the most successful societal planning efforts in modern times. This should not be made light of, just because the more distant, greater philosophical picture remains unaltered thereby. The fact that women, minorities, the poor and small languages can all achieve vernacular literacy nowadays is enough of a triumph to satisfy most criteria of equity between sociocultures, albeit huge gaps in other respects (other than literacy) doubtlessly remain to be tackled.

Reference

Fishman, J.A. (ed.) (1971) *Advances in the Sociology of Language* (Vol. 1). The Hague: Mouton.

Index

Afrikaans, 46, 49, 78
Alexander, Neville, 77
Alighierre, Dante, 52
Anglo-Saxon, 20, 24, 27, 37
– eclipse, 25
Arabic, 20, 27, 38, 73, 81
– importation, 47–48
– modernization, 27
Asturian, 49, 81
– vs. Spanish, 11
Attributes
– rank-order progression, 14–15
Ausbau, 49–50
Australia English literacy, 78
Authority, 2
Autonomy, 15t, 16

Bantu, 78
Beowulf, 20
Berber writings, 44
Bible, 39
Bik, Shmul, 63
Burkina Faso Internet, 83n
Bulgarian vs. Macedonian, 11

Canada English literacy, 75–76, 77
Cape Verdean, 82
Carthage, 44
Castilian, 40
Chinese, 44, 73
Christian clergy, 51
Churches, 38. See also European vernacular literacy heroes
Classical literacy, 20, 21, 27, 37
Classical status attainment, 16
Clergy, 20, 51
Code varieties, 16–17
Communication instrumentalities growth, 70
Computers maintaining small languages, 7
Creole, 16

Demotic, 50n
de Nebrija, Antonio, 51–52, 84

Deutsch, Karl W., 19–20
Dialects, 6, 16, 42–43, 49, 77
– lacking perspectival autonomy, 11–12
Dictionary standardization, 12
Dreams, 84
Dutch, 11–12, 25, 27, 49, 81
– vs. Frisian, 11

Econotechnical and sociocultural change, 14
English, 25, 27
– age, 9, 73
– change-resistant features, 1–2
– changes, 1
– defense, 63
– illiteracy, 31
– modernization, 46
– orthographic inconsistencies, 2
– pidgin, 74–75
– record keeping, 13
– regard, 3
– religion, 37–39
– South Africa, 49
– spelling irregularity, 11
– Tanzania, 82
English literacy
– exportation and Anglosphere indigenous vernacular literacy, 73–78
– Puerto Rico vs. India, 76–77
Entrepreneurship, 68–69
European elites, 66–67
European literacy
– geographic occurrences, 32–33
– spread, 32, 34
– tracing course, 20
– vernaculars in 950 to 1990, 22t–23t
European map, 33f
European vernacular
– competitors with local vernacular literacies, 80–83
– literacy, 29
European vernacular literacy heroes, 51–65
– Antonio de Nebrija (1441–1552), 51–52
– Four Horsemen, 64–65

– Johann Gutenberg (1390–1468), 53–55
– Mendl Lefin (1749–1826), 60–63
– Vuk Stefanovic Karadzic (1787–1864), 56–59

Failure, 84
Ferguson, Charles A., 51
Folkloric material, 59–60, 62, 67
Formal education, 30
Four Horsemen, 64–65
French, 24–25, 27, 40, 42–43, 73–75
– age, 9
– cultural dominance, 54
– literacy, 77, 79–80
– Luxembourg, 49
– political and cultural policy, 79
– spelling, 11
Frisian vs. Dutch, 11

Germanic-Romanic spoken language border, 42
Germany, 9, 11, 20–21, 24–28, 37–49, 56–57, 81
– divide, 33
– Lefin, 62–63
– literacy, 54
– Reformation, 56–57
– sociocultural conservatism, 38
– vs. Spain, 54
– united political center, 37
– Vuk, 58–61
Gramatica Castellans (de Nebrija), 52
Greek, 20, 27, 31, 58
Greek vernaculars, 30–31, 50
Guarani, 81
Gutenberg, Johann, 52–56, 60, 64, 69
– Bible, 4, 52
– Latin books, 56

Hebrew, 20, 27, 47, 60
– modernization, 62, 63–64
Highly reproducible scale, 15t
Hindi vs. Urdu, 11
Hindustani, 47–48
Historicity, 15t
Human speech variation, 10
Hungarian, 27, 57–58

IAL. *See* International Auxiliary Language (IAL)
Intercontinental trade, 45–46
Interdependence, 2–3
International Auxiliary Language (IAL), 16–17

Israeli, 50
Italian, 9, 24–25, 27, 81

Judaism, 60–62

Karadzic, Vuk Stefanovic, 56–59, 84
Khasidim, 61
Kopitar, Jerney, 59
Kurdish, 83n

Language
– age, 8–9
– co-causal influence, 48
– contextually conditioned impact, 41
– deaths, 13
– number of speakers, 7
– older varieties vs. younger varieties, 8–9
– recent increase in interest, 1–5
– social change, 13
– spoken variety, 5
– subsidiary varieties, 6
– uniformation, 9–10
– variety usage societal views, 41
– within-community attitudes, 6–7
Language of vernacular literacy defined, 5–18
– dictionary definition, 5
– scalability, 14–18
Lateness to literacy, 48
Latin, 20, 40, 56–57
– alphabets, 71
– distance, 37
– Gutenberg's books, 56
– Nebrija's first works, 52
– precursor language, 9
– rejection, 39
– vernaculars, 26, 30–32, 47
Law no. 94–665 of 4 August 1994, 79
Lefin, Mendl, 60–63, 84
Letzembourgish, 49–50
Lifelong learning, 18
Literacy
– appropriate, 48
– definition, 18
– functional adult minimum level, 18
– lateness, 48
– learning time, 30
– outcomes, 85
– promises, 3
– recent increase in interest, 1–5
– redundancy, 30
– revealed intercultural languages, 30
– small and nonliterate populations, 14
– spread, 3, 26–27

Index

– state efforts, 80
Literacy bullies on block, 73–83
– Anglosphere indigenous vernacular literacy, 73–78
– English literacy exportation, 73–78
– European vernaculars, 80–83
– vernacular literacies comparison, 79
Literarization, 31
Little languages along Rhine, 43
'Loi Toubon' (Law no. 94–665 of 4 August 1994), 79
Luxembourg, 49

Macedonian *vs.* Bulgarian, 11
Many languages, 7
Maskilim, 61
Mass vernacular literacy introduction, 34t
Mind modernization, 2
Minority languages, 29
Modern wars, 29
Mozambique, 82

National American Literacy Survey (NALS), 18
National communication study, 19
Nationalism and Social Communication (Deutsch), 20
Norwegian, 24–25, 27, 86

Occitan, 40
Old Church Slavonic, 20, 37, 47, 57
Old Saxon, 9
Oral feedback, 10
Oral vernaculars, 24
Oudet, Maurice, 83n

Pagan varieties, 20
Pennsylfanisch, 47
Pidgin, 80
– English, 74–75
– lack of attributable front, 17
– progression to creole, 16
Polish, 27
Popular literacy, 29
– arrival, 19
Popular vernacular European literacy
– beginning, 21
– spatial/geographic arrival, 35
Popular vernacular literature, 55–56
Portuguese, 24–27, 40, 81, 82
Printing press, 4, 52, 65
– invention, 54–55
Protestantism, 38–39
Provençal, 40

Puerto Rico, 5, 79, 81
– English literacy, 75–76

Quechua/Quichua, 81

Reformation, 55–56
Religion
– literacy, 38–39
– social change, 40
Religious semiclassicals, 39
Republic of South Africa, 77
Reward systems, 86
Rhine, 43
Roman local vernaculars, 32
Romance literacy vernaculars, 25, 27
Russian, 11, 24–25, 27, 58–62
– recognition, 73

Scalability position change, 16
Serbia, 56–60, 84
Slang, 5
Small languages, 7
Snow, C.P., 56
Social behavior scalable properties, 15
Social change, 47
Societal process variables, 35
Southern English, 5
Spanish, 27, 40, 73, 75–76, 84
– abroad, 81–82
– *vs.* Asturian, 11
– *vs.* German, 54
– grammar, 52–53
– popular literacy, 52–53
– recognition, 73
– vernacular literacy, 84
Spanish Africa (Sahara), 81
Spoken communication, 10, 21
Standardization, 2, 15t, 16
Swahili, 82n
Swedish, 81
Syncretistic religious varieties, 20

Tanzania, 46, 79, 82n
Textual sacralization, 39
Transborder arrangements, 43
Turkish, 27, 58

Ukrainian, 11, 49
United States, 15, 45–46
– English literacy, 76–78
– Spanish, 81–82
Urdu *vs.* Hindi, 11

Vade mecum, 3

Variety of languages, 6–7
- regional differences, 25–26
Vernacular literacy
- Anglosphere *vs.* Francosphere attitudes, 79–80
- *vs.* classicals of literacy, 37
- introduction to European Continent, 34t
- purpose, 84–87
- road to heaven littered with good intentions, 85–86
- societal change, 28–29
Vernacular literacy rise in Europe, 19–36
- Karl W. Deutsch (1912–1992) and Time 1 (T1), 19–20
- Time 2 (T2) 1250 C.E. and next few centuries, 21–26
- Time 3 (T3) 1800 C.E., 27
- Time 4 (T4) 1900, 28
- Times 5 and 6 (T5 and T6) 1937 and 1990, 28–29
- understanding literacy society-wide characteristics, 30–36
Vernacular literacy societal spread macro-factors, 37–50

- dampening effects, 48–50
- literacy rise, 45
- nonreligious pursuits, 40–44
- religions of literacy, 37–39
- spread of religion, philosophy and style of life, 46–47
- West to East trajectory in vernacular languages, 45
- widespread sociocultural change, 40–44
Vernacular literacy societal spread micro-factors, 66–72
- chicken and egg problem, 69
- elephant in room growth, 70
- elitist literacy and outgrowths, 66–68
- parsimonious communicational possibilities, 70
Vitality, 15t, 24
Vuk. *See* Karadzic, Vuk Stefanovic

Westernization combined with cultural ethnonationalism, 59
World War II, 29

Yiddish, 27, 47, 60–63

For Product Safety Concerns and Information please contact our EU Authorised Representative:

Easy Access System Europe

Mustamäe tee 50

10621 Tallinn

Estonia

gpsr.requests@easproject.com

www.ingramcontent.com/pod-product-compliance
Ingram Content Group UK Ltd.
Pitfield, Milton Keynes, MK11 3LW, UK
UKHW021830140426
5217IPUK00021B/1373